The PLUGGED-IN PARENT ALMANAC 2023

The PLUGGED-IN PARENT ALMANAC 2023

The Guide to Popular Culture for Parents of Tweens and Teens

Edited by
ANJA SCHMIDT

PARENT **READY**

PARENT READY

Parent Ready
8 East Windsor Avenue
Alexandria, Virginia 22301
https://parentready.com

Copyright © 2023 by Parent Ready, Inc.

Parent Ready supports the right to free expression and the value of copyright. The purpose of copyright is to encourage the creation of works that enrich our culture.

All rights reserved. No part of this book may be reprinted or reproduced in any form or by any electronic, mechanical, or other means, now known or hereafter invented, including photocopying, recording, and information storage and retrieval, without the prior written permission of the publisher, except in the case of brief quotations embodied in critical articles and reviews.

First Parent Ready trade paperback edition January 2022

Parent Action and design are trademarks of Parent Ready, Inc.

Bulk purchase special discounts are available.
Please make inquiries via www.pluggedinparent.guide.

Interior illustrations by Frank Caruso
Interior design by Jason Snyder

Library of Congress Cataloging-in-Publication Data has been applied for.

ISBN: 979-8-9880158-0-2

CONTENTS

HELLO PARENTS!...8

What Teens Wish Parents Knew!...10

PART I

Pop Culture Know-How

HOW DOES SOMETHING
BECOME POPULAR?...12

The Big Universes...16

THE IMPORTANCE OF POP CULTURE
IN YOUR CHILD'S LIFE...17

When Will My Child Be Interested In...22

THE CONVERSATION: TALKING
ABOUT MEDIA USE & BEHAVIORS...23

Digital Safety & Responsibility...27

Pop Culture Events Teens Are Looking Forward To...28

PART II

Teen Passions & Actions

How Do Teens Spend Their Time?...30

CONNECT

Social Media Platforms

A PARENT'S GUIDE TO
SOCIAL MEDIA PLATFORMS...32

What in the World is a Meme?...34

PLAY

Games

BREAKING DOWN THE WORLD OF VIDEO GAMES...42

You Say "Multiverse" & I Say "Metaverse"...48

UNPLUG YOUR KIDS: RECOMMENDATIONS FROM TOY STORE OWNER MICHAEL TIMKO...49

WATCH

Movies, Series & Specials

Top Streaming Television Series & Movies...54

WHAT TO WATCH ON TV WITH YOUR TEEN...57

HOW TO TALK TO YOUR KID ABOUT...ZOMBIES. (& DESCENDANTS) (& ALSO SYSTEMIC INEQUALITY)...64

Why Kids Like to Be Scared...69

READ

YA Franchises & Fan Fiction

Top Young Adult Franchises & Novels...72

A PARENT'S GUIDE TO FAN FICTION...76

ANIME & MANGA: THROUGH THE LENS OF OUR CHILDREN...82

Best Anime Series for Beginners...85

CONNECTING WITH YOUR KIDS THROUGH COMIC BOOKS...87

PLUGGED-IN PARENT SUMMER CHALLENGE...94

LISTEN

Music

UNDERSTANDING TODAY'S POP MUSIC...100

WHY LIVE MUSIC MATTERS...105

Survey: Favorite Musicians, Bands & Groups...108

COLLECT & TRADE

COLLECTING: WE'RE BEYOND THE CHECKLIST. WAY BEYOND...110

WHAT DO KIDS COLLECT & TRADE?...114

Marketplaces...115

A TEENAGER'S GUIDE TO SNEAKER CULTURE...118

SHOW OFF A STYLE

Beauty & Fashion

A PARENT'S GUIDE TO FASHION & BEAUTY TRENDS...124

Top Fashion & Beauty Retailers for Teens...132

GET TO KNOW BEAUTY INFLUENCERS...134

THE COST OF RAISING A TEENAGER...140

Survey: Birthday Gifts...153

GLOSSARY...154

CONTRIBUTORS...170

HELLO PARENTS!

If you've picked up this book, you are probably getting ready to, or are in the midst of, parenting a teenager. And let's be frank, this will be one of the hardest stages of your life.

Oh sure, we've experienced the stressfulness of our own teenage years. Teenage angst is real. It's developmentally appropriate. But it's nothing when compared to the angst we, as parents, feel.

According to Laurence Steinberg, a Temple University psychologist, "It doesn't seem to me like adolescence is a difficult time for the kids. Most adolescents seem to be going through life in a very pleasant haze."

But he says, "It's when I talk to the parents that I notice something. If you look at the narrative, it's 'my teenager who's driving me crazy.'"

One thing that's very hard for parents is to keep up with the pop culture that consumes so much of our kids' attention, the focus of their passions that becomes part of their identity.

But that's part of our job as parents. And this volume will help you transcend the adolescent entertainment upheaval that might be taking over your household.

If you are the parent of a soon-to-be teen, this volume will help you acclimate to an entirely new world that is calling out to your teen. If you already have a teen in your household, this volume will help you get ready for the year ahead. And if you are an educator or other professional who interacts with teens every day, this volume will help you understand what they are talking about a little bit better.

HELLO PARENTS!

Our purpose is not to make you cool. Please don't try to be cool. Parents are not supposed to be cool (at least not all of the time).

We do hope to help you avoid some eye rolls and sarcastic comments.

Most importantly, we hope to help you connect better with your child. Stories and entertainment have long brought people together. Pop culture makers have certainly leveraged teens' need for discovery and independence into massive commercial opportunity. And since Elvis and the Beatles (if not before), discord has often been created between generations as well.

Today's fractured and fluid pop culture environment has created much more of a generational divide. Parents don't even get the chance to express abhorrence or dismay about the newest celebrity. Rather, we're frequently just clueless.

This is not a bible of pop culture. Our hope is to provide you with a glimpse into the pop culture world so that you have a chance to communicate your values and share in the joy and wonder of today's creators.

Across genre and platform, we provide you with a road map to the year ahead in pop culture. Surprise is a big part of what makes pop culture attractive. So, we will not even try to pretend that we have a crystal ball about all of the hits and headlines. But we can help you identify the big landmarks and way stations and make the teenage pop culture world a little less confusing.

We are inspired in this endeavor by *The Old Farmer's Almanac*, whose purpose is to be "useful, with a pleasant sense of humor." We hope you have fun reading this book. We also hope you'll use this information to have more enjoyable dinner-time conversations and to create memories that will support your parent-child relationships for a lifetime!

—*The Editors*

WHAT TEENS WISH PARENTS KNEW!

It's hard for parents to get their teens to speak openly to them. Take a breath. It's completely normal. Pulling away from parents is part of adolescent development. To provide our readers with some insight into what teens might want their parents to know if they *actually told them*, Plugged-In Parent surveyed 213 teens between the ages of 13 and 17. This isn't a statistically significant survey. But the responses will provide you with a perspective and could be used to start a conversation with your teens. Other results of the survey are sprinkled throughout this year's *Almanac*.

TikTok

Everything; they don't know anything

Anything

Clothing and sneakers

That it's not all bad

How games work

Anime

That not every song is about sex and drugs

That every black rapper isn't a gangster

You can't pause online games

What it is

That it isn't as dangerous as they make it seem

KPOP

That it's just a bunch of jokes and barely anything should be taken seriously

Times are changing

Memes

That not everything on the internet is true

"Well, how truly fun it is sometimes"

That teenagers aren't always on their phones

Movies

They know everything already (sarcasm intended)

Music

To be open to concepts of difference and acceptance of people not straight or cis-gendered

Source: *Plugged-In Parent Survey of Teens*

PART I:
Pop Culture Know-How

HOW DOES SOMETHING BECOME POPULAR?

By Meredith Levine

The word "popular" can conjure meaning for anyone of any age, whether it is in reference to the most popular person in school, popular culture, a popular style or restaurant. When we think of things "becoming popular," we think of them as becoming well-liked within a certain group of people and, in some cases, well-known amongst a broader group of people.

Popular conjures the idea of people clamoring to be close to, spend time with, get to know, and/or consume, the subject.

So how does something become both well-liked and well-known in a community?

More often than not, it is a blend of word-of-mouth praise and the ability to connect with others who have similar tastes.

The internet was *made* to do this. So, what does the Popularity Process look like?

1. Personally **discovering** something
2. **Enjoying** or getting curious about it
3. **Connecting** to other people who are open about liking it
4. Liking it together **without shame**
5. **Becoming a source** for other people to discover it
6. Watching **loop** repeat with a new person

These cycles may be brief, like a TikTok trend, or more evergreen, like a video game or franchise universe.

TIKTOK TRENDS

In the case of a TikTok trend, there is a lot of algorithmic intervention that both prompts discovery—TikTok sees something gaining traction among popular users in a community and serves them more of whatever that is—and the ability for a loop to form (thus expanding the trend's reach). When a TikTok trend has run its course (i.e., hits a community that isn't reacting as positively to it or that doesn't understand the joke), users send cues to TikTok to squash the reach (i.e., marking a video "not interested" or hiding a creator). TikTok also benefits from having fast trend cycles because it keeps people exposed to new content—thus combating boredom—a key factor about the platform's appeal. This is why if users participate in trends too late, TikTok doesn't always achieve the reach needed for a loop to form successfully.

So on TikTok, both the ability to discover something new and the extent to which it can get looped is largely controlled by algorithms and informed by user behavior.

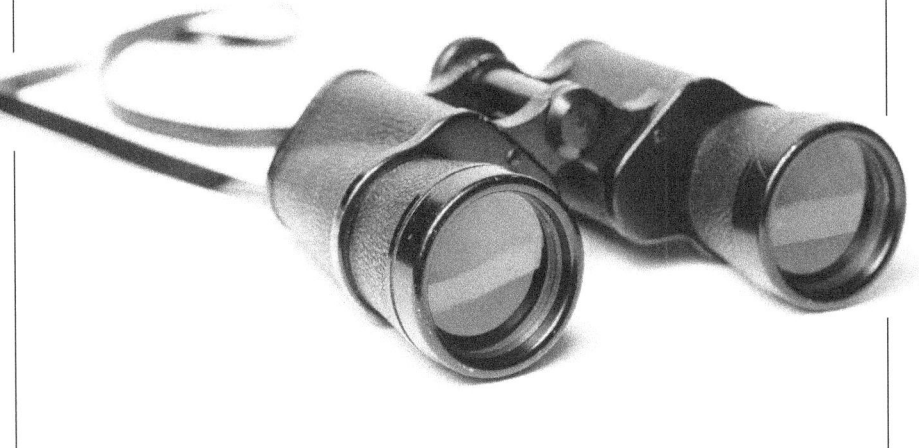

EVERGREEN TRENDS

In the case of something more evergreen, there are a couple of nuanced paths:

1. Things that were not popular when they came out but have become more popular over time (think Dungeons & Dragons)

2. Things that felt like instant hits (think Minecraft or Taylor Swift)

In the first case of unpopular things becoming popular, the barriers to the Popularity Process were not always in steps 1 or 2, as libraries, bookstores, and comic book shops have been a source for discovery and learning or enjoying. The challenges were in steps 3–5.

The instant hits tend to reach more mainstream audiences upon launch and have less of an uphill battle to face in terms of overcoming shame enough to become a point of discovery for new people to discover it, and thus becoming a loop.

Over the pandemic, we saw jigsaw puzzles go from a sleeper hit that people quietly did at home and with their families (but never talked about lest they get viewed as "boring") to a hobby in its own right, with Facebook groups, Reddit threads, and Instagram creators devoted to the meditative act of puzzle-solving, as well as an uptick in puzzle exchanges and conversations about the quality of puzzles. These communities formed both out of passion (typically online) and out of proximity (local puzzle swaps).

POPULARITY IN CONTEXT

For kids who enjoy things that their proximal peers may not, there is always the internet to turn to—to share in the inside jokes of a smaller, or different, community than the ones parents may typically think of. Popular subjects may appear on a text chain of close friends, among a group at school, or as commercially successful in a city, state, country, or the world. Popularity may feel like a universal truth, especially for young people, but the reality is that popular things are *contextually* popular.

New things become popular as kids age, as culture changes, as contexts change. We popularize things that resonate with us, reflect our shared values, or provide the experiences we are seeking (often this is the need for self-soothing, identity building, or community building).

Young people become beacons for *the thing* that reflects who they are, who their friends are, and who they strive to be. Sometimes these things stay popular for an individual, a community, or a society, and sometimes they change as people enter new cycles of discovery and connection. It's important to ask your child what they're finding popular—as an insight into who they are becoming as individuals, what values they are building, and what experiences they are seeking out.

Meredith Levine is a fanthropologist professionally studying culture and its fans for the last 10+ years.

The Big Universes

They may have started as a comic book, or perhaps as a novel. Maybe even as a board game. But the idea of stories and characters that span different mediums isn't new. We now live in a time when stories and characters from a few big fictional universes dominate attention across movies, video games, books, merchandise, and even fashion.

Some kids might continue their fandom for a universe into their teens or they might develop new passions.

The largest universes that will sure draw attention in the coming year are:

- Marvel Cinematic Universe
- The DC Universe
- Harry Potter
- Star Wars
- Dungeons & Dragons
- Game of Thrones
- Anime
- Magic: The Gathering
- Supernatural
- My Little Pony

THE IMPORTANCE OF POP CULTURE IN YOUR CHILD'S LIFE

By Henry Jenkins

Let's start with some basic premises. Popular culture is an ordinary aspect of our everyday lives, something we live with and work around. We deploy resources from popular culture to express our identities and connect with (or signal our differences from) other people in our lives. As parents, we should be less concerned with what media is doing to our children than with what our children are doing with media.

HOW OUR CHILDREN USE MEDIA

The continuities are greater than the differences. Young people listen to different bands and often acquire music through different platforms than teens did a few decades ago, yet one's taste in music is still a key indicator of social identity. Young people play different games on different platforms yet young people still acquire and display mastery through competitive play much as their parents who grew up playing Pac-Man or Super Mario Bros. Young people use different social networking platforms, yet forging a place for oneself within the social system of their schools remains a central goal of adolescence. Many new digital practices that seem alien to older people are serving purposes which, if they are being honest, they recognize from their own teen experiences.

That said, there are also significant differences. Today's grandparents grew up in an era of three major networks, ABC, NBC, and CBS. Today's parents grew up alongside the proliferation of cable networks. But today's children inhabit a streaming media ecology where they control what media they consume—when, where, and how—more than ever before. Consequently, those media choices more fully reflect their personal tastes and social affiliations.

Young people play active roles in this new media landscape. Most have produced some content, even if only sharing photographs via social media. Most know people who are making even more media content than they are, which further helps to normalize media production as part of their everyday lives. Young people also play an active role in shaping the circulation and publicity of media content they find meaningful, embedding it into a social life that is defined through their ability to maintain immediate contact with their friends as a support system

- as they move through their day
- to remain connected with their peers, no matter where they are
- to form intense, intimate social ties with people who they may never meet face-to-face but with whom they share cultural preferences.

Influencers are often not simply niche celebrities but may be people with whom they have regular contact and even hubs for their own communities of participants.

EXPANDING THEIR WORLDS THROUGH MEDIA

In the streaming media age, young people are constantly scanning their environments for interesting new media options, which might surface at any moment and from anywhere in the world. They are pop cosmopolitans, escaping what they see as the parochialism of their own culture by consuming pop culture from elsewhere around the world. K-pop, Anime, Bollywood, Telenovelas, and the like become part of their entry into a multicultural society. Pop cosmopolitans co-exist with diaspora communities who are accelerating the flow of media across national borders as a means of connecting back to their homelands. Prior generations rarely saw television that was not produced by our own domestic industry—perhaps British content on public television or low budget syndicated series from

POP CULTURE KNOW-HOW

Canada—whereas Netflix has a steady stream (pun intended) of foreign language successes, such as *Squid Game* (Korea), *The Witcher* (Poland), *or Lupin* (France).

Significant stories often depend on sprawling transmedia storyworlds, place a strong premium on fan investment and expertise, and reward re-viewings. Think about Star Wars or the Marvel universe, each with installments as films, television series, video games, novels, comic books, and amusement park attractions. When they find something that matters to them, youth drill deep into that universe's vast recesses, hoping to lose themselves in its winding narrative paths. In these immersive worlds, youth are hunters and gatherers who get bragging rights by finding new content and bringing it back to their tribe, as well as by forming fan theories that predict future developments or model fresh interpretations.

They may also find themselves through an infinitely proliferating set of pop music subgenres, which they can make their own through remixes and memes, dance and lip-sync performances, blog posts and podcasts.

And youth around the world are protesting in the streets against gun violence, wealth inequality, climate change, or racism and sexism, using a vernacular of wizards, zombies, handmaidens, and superheroes, drawn from popular culture—much as an earlier generation might have drawn metaphors from the Bible as they fought for civil rights. Again, popular culture offers them the stories they use to define their identities and make sense of the world around them, so it makes sense that these same stories would be foundational to their civic imagination—to the ways they articulate their visions for a better future or their fears about a threatening world.

GET ENGAGED

No matter how strange or unfamiliar all of this may seem on the surface, please understand that these choices and practices are meaningful to your child. The best way to learn what all of this means to them is to *ask* them, to engage in conversations that *take their choices seriously*, and to *keep an open mind*.

HENRY JENKINS is the Provost Professor of Communication, Journalism, Cinematic Arts and Education at the University of Southern California.

Practical Strategies, Tips and Tools to Support Your Student's Success

The Parents' Guide to Studying and Learning is an easy-to-use companion for parents to help their students truly learn and get better grades.

Learn more at **studyandlearn.guide**

Published by

parentready.com

When will my child be interested in...

Using TikTok?	9–11
Using Snapchat?	9–11
Wearing makeup?	9–11
Hating their parents?	9–13
Owning a smartphone?	11–12
Using curse words?	11–12
Developing an identity outside of their role in the family?	11–14
How they look and dress?	12–14
Spending up to 9 hours a day using a screen?	12+
Getting a social media account? (Instagram, Twitter, etc.)	13–15
Listening to their own music?	13–15
Being friends with members of the opposite sex?	14–16
Romantic relationships and sexuality?	14–16
Exploring or trying on different types of identities?	14–18
Taking stronger stances on moral or ethical issues?	14–18
Career-related activities?	14–18
Making friends online?	15–17
Instant/online messaging their friends?	15–17
Watching or getting involved in online/social media drama?	15–17
Having friends beyond a single clique?	17–19

(Not tweens/teens, but still interesting...)

Watching YouTube	3–4
Using a tablet	3–4
Using a computer	5–8
Using a gaming device	5–8
Talking to Siri or Alexa	5–8

THE CONVERSATION
Talking About Media Use & Behaviors

By Emily Weinstein & Carrie James

Adults can fall into the trap of thinking that if we're not in the loop, we're so out of it that we have nothing to offer to our teens' conversations. *Who is Jack Harlow? Who is Doja Cat? I don't even know how to start the conversation, let alone what to say.*

We've spent the last decade talking to teens and families about social media and we can tell you three things for sure:

1. You do have wisdom that your kid needs to thrive in a digital world (even if you've never heard of influencers like Jack Harlow and Doja Cat).

2. We set our families up for success when we think of ourselves more like coaches and less like referees.

3. Effective support starts with asking instead of assuming.

Let's tackle these three points in reverse order.

TABLE ASSUMPTIONS & ASK QUESTIONS

The news is filled with fear-inducing headlines about social media that can seem to confirm our deepest fears. It's true that social media can amplify issues for teens, and make difficult issues even harder. But what's difficult for one kid is different for another, and social media isn't all negative. When adults assume we know what's going on and/or assume it's all dire, we miss a golden opportunity to connect with our kids. We also miss out on chances to build the kind of trust and open communication that is essential so that kids will come to us when issues arise ("Hey Dad, someone just sent this inappropriate picture to our group chat, what should I do?").

Make it a routine to prioritize open-ended questions as a starting point. These kinds of questions tee-up better, richer tech conversations. A few of our favorites are:

- What's best about growing up with today's technologies?
- What makes it difficult?
- What worries you most about social media?
- When do you feel best or most inspired?
- Can you tell me about the moments when social media makes you feel lonely or insecure?

COACH, DON'T REFEREE

If we see our primary job as doling out screen time minutes and blowing the whistle when kids are over time, we take on the role of tech referee. The same is true if we just enforce penalties for rule-breaking and assume our job is done. The reality is that today's technologies are intentionally designed with features that make it extremely difficult to pull away. This is true for all of us, but especially for adolescents who are still developing the abilities for self-regulation. Learning how to manage life with technology is hard!

Good coaches help their players understand the rules of the game. They also help players learn skills they need and put them into practice under pressure. Good coaches are allies in

THE CONVERSATION

challenging moments, right there to help players come up with a plan.

Be clear with your kid about your goals for them when it comes to technology. This might mean saying things like:

▸ "You should use this device to connect with me when we're apart, and it's my job to make sure it isn't disconnecting our family when we're together. That means we have rules like no phones in the room during meals. I am going to follow this rule, too."

▸ "Sleep is really important and I know it can be especially hard to pull away at night, so our family rule is phones in the kitchen or completely turned off by 10 p.m." Or whatever time works for your family.

▸ "You can use this device to connect with friends, but it's never okay to use it to be mean to others." (For younger kids, you may want to add: "Nothing you say over text is private and I'm going to check your messages once in a while to help you remember that other kids' parents might be checking theirs, too. I'm checking in and on your phone more now—but I'll always tell you when and why. As you get older, you'll have more privacy.")

A good coach knows when to pull a player from the game altogether, but this move is typically a last resort. We appreciate this way of thinking because the cost of disconnection can be really high, especially for teens. This doesn't mean it's never warranted, like when kids are in crisis and social media is very clearly exacerbating the problem. But our aim for most teens, most of the time, is to help them learn how to participate in a digital world in ways that are developmentally appropriate and supportive of their well-being.

FIND THE FAMILIAR

It's true that social media is changing the game in many ways, but it's also the case that the core challenges and emotions kids are facing usually have familiar roots—familiar to when we were growing up. In painful moments, the underlying feelings are often age-old struggles like insecurity, body worries, feeling left out, concerns about reputation, heightened anxiety about what peers think, wanting to be liked, and so on. These developmental needs predate apps, though it's fair to say social media apps can amplify them in real ways.

If your teen is panicked because she sees on a Snapmap that her friends' avatars are together in one place, don't worry that you don't know what a Snapmap is. Focus on the experience of being left out, and tap into the empathy and wisdom you have around what helps. What would you want someone to say if you were excluded by your friends? Your teen needs your core wisdom and empathy much more than they need a tech-savvy parent.

DRS. EMILY WEINSTEIN and **CARRIE JAMES** are researchers who have worked for over a decade studying youth and technology at Project Zero, a research center at the Harvard Graduate School of Education.

Digital Safety & Responsibility

Parents should take matters of digital safety and responsibility seriously.

And just like the need to prepare our children for other aspects of adult life (looking forward to those driving lessons?), we need to help our children navigate the turmoil that is often social media. And it is critical to remain connected while doing so.

The federal Cybersecurity and Infrastructure Security Agency and the nonprofit Common Sense Media provide comprehensive resources to help parents keep up on the latest in safety best practices.

 checkology®

A future
founded on facts

Young people are navigating the most complex information landscape in human history.

Truth, evidence and facts compete for attention alongside rumors, hoaxes, misinformation and disinformation.

Education is the solution.

News literacy is a vital life skill. Our Checkology® virtual classroom helps students determine what information they can trust, share and act on.

Try our FREE resource:
get.checkology.org

POP CULTURE EVENTS TEENS ARE LOOKING FORWARD TO

TV Shows   New Music
Concerts   A better year than 2021
Adele concert   AnimeCon   NBA Final
New Kpop Groups   Comic Con
Game Awards   VidCon   A new lil baby album
Grammys   Makeup Collabs
Met Gala   Super Bowl   Oscars   World Cup
Off White Clothing   Marvel Movies

Source: *Plugged-In Parent Survey of Teens*

PART II:
Teen Passions & Actions

How Do Teens Spend Their Time?

ACTIVITY	AVG TIME SPENT (ALL)	AVG TIME BOYS	AVG TIME GIRLS
Sleeping	9h 43m	9h 48m	9h 38m
Screen time (phone, gaming, TV, surfing the web)	7h 22m	7h 36m	7h 7m
Class time	3h 32m	3h 45m	3h 18m
Listening to music	2h 5m		
Socializing with friends (extracuricculars, parties, events, phone calls, hanging out)	1h 13m	1h 5m	1h 22m
Eating	1h 5m	1h 2m	1h 9m
Homework	1h	50m	1h 11m
Grooming (bathing, getting dressed, haircuts, etc.)	51m	40m	1h 3m
Playing sports	45m	59m	33m
Chores	31m	24m	38m
Paid work	26m	27m	24m
Volunteering/taking care of others (unpaid)	25m	19m	30m
Errands (groceries, etc.)	16m	11m	21m
Shopping (buying clothes, going to the mall)	10m	5m	15m

CONNECT
Social Media Platforms

A PARENT'S GUIDE TO SOCIAL MEDIA PLATFORMS

From Instagram and TikTok to Steam and Twitch, there are numerous ways for kids to connect online with their friends. We've compiled a guide to some of the most popular social media platforms for Gen Zers.

TIKTOK

Not a clock, not a ticking time bomb, but a social media platform that specializes in videos, currently lasting up to three minutes. If you noticed your kids' attention span suddenly (and oddly) increasing this past year, perhaps it's due in part to TikTok making its second video length limit extension, from 60 seconds to 3 minutes. This is 12 times the original limit length of 15 seconds.

TikTok allows users to create, share, and comment on videos. Additionally, users can tag their friends, ensuring everyone is in the know. With almost a billion users globally, TikTok was the most downloaded app in 2020. As of mid-2021, it remains so. With so many users, it's no surprise that there's all sorts of mainstream content, which most users refer to

Top-Earning TikTok Influencers (U.S.)

Charli D'Amelio
Dixie D'Amelio
Addison Rae
Bella Poarch
Josh Richards
Kris Collins
Avani Gregg

Source: *Forbes*

as Straight TikTok (think of the dancing videos initially associated with TikTok). And yet, what makes this app lauded among the younger crowd is its subcultures. If your kid loves frogs, for example, perhaps they've found Frog TikTok, a subgenre of the Elite, or Alt, TikTok community that is accessed after a user views many videos about a particular topic.

INSTAGRAM

If you didn't take a picture of it, did it really happen? We reckon you've heard your kid say this; perhaps you've even said it yourself. The app that allows users to edit, share, and comment on photos has branched out to include videos, a story feature, and live streaming. With all the digital editing tools at their fingertips, it's no wonder the phrase Instagram "model" now refers to a real profession and a popular insult. Instagram models are like influencers—self-represented people who promote various brands.

We'd be remiss not to mention Finsta, short for Fake Instagram. Before you pull a Senator Blumenthal, you should know your kid may have more than one account on which they share different aspects of themselves. No, it's not separate from Instagram or even a side of Instagram. It's simply how kids refer to each other's more candid and unfiltered accounts.

> **Top Instagram Influencers (U.S.)**
> *@selenagomez*
> *@therock*
> *@arianagrande*
> *@kendalljenner*
> *@khloekardashian*
> *@jlo*
> *@taylorswift*
> *@katyperry*
> *@kyliejenner*
> Source: #heepsy

What in the World is a Meme?

Has your child ever said anything witty? Have they made an interesting observation? Well, why not ask them if they've considered turning that idea into a meme? It's super easy and free to create a meme. Adobe Creative Cloud Express offers a meme generator with templates where one can create their own header, background, and totally customize its look. Canva offers a similar tool. What's hard is coming up with the timely ironic or sarcastic insight that will get attention. (Or one can always try cute cats!) Once created, one can upload their meme to GIPHY, Know Your Meme, Tumblr, or Reddit to hope it gets noticed.

Following are the popular types of meme humor to get your child started!

1. **"Classic" memes** were most popular from the mid-2000s to the 2010s, with today's youth considering them somewhat cringey. Classic memes are based around kids, parenting, pets, and everyday life and are straightforward in their messaging.

2. A **dank,** or **spicy, meme** is an ironic expression used to describe online viral media and in-jokes that are intentionally bizarre or have become cliché. In this context, the word "dank," originally coined as a term for high-quality marijuana, is satirically used as a synonym for "cool," but your tween might not know this and just describe the memes as "brain-dead" or "stupid."

3. **Deep fried memes** are made from an image that is run through so many filters that it becomes grainy, washed-out, or oddly colored, often to the point that it is humorously hard to make out. They are usually accompanied with a silly caption.

CONNECT

4. In an **exploitable meme,** a single image is manipulated through various means to achieve a humorous effect. This can involve replacing words in the original image, adding words to the original image, or manipulating positions of objects in the image to change the original's meaning. Exploitables became popular because they can be edited with basic programs such as MS Paint or Photoshop.

5. **Reaction images** are images or animated gifs that portray a specific emotion in response to something that has been said, such as emoticons. They are often used as to make fun of how others react to common situations.

6. A **catchphrase** is a recognizable expression, frequently used online and off. Catchphrases can be associated with a particular image or video but are typically well-known enough that they may appear as part of other memes.

7. **Text-based memes** consist primarily of text, either by itself (such as screenshots of Tweets shared on Instagram or Facebook) or placed on a gradient background or low-quality photo. The text might be a joke, political or social commentary, or something more silly.

TEEN PASSIONS & ACTIONS

SNAPCHAT

Snapchat is like texting but with photos and short videos called *snaps*, all of which immediately poof into the electronic ether after viewed, unless the photo or video is part of the user's story, which lasts 24 hours and has a variable level of viewership depending on the user's privacy settings. Users can respond to snaps from friends with another snap, or with words.

Your kid can also create groups with their friends. Word chats disappear too, avoiding screenshots. But as any veteran snap chatter knows, screenshots are always possible, if one's fingers are quick enough.

Besides keeping in touch with their friends, kids may also follow their idols—from actors and musicians to professional footballers and chess players.

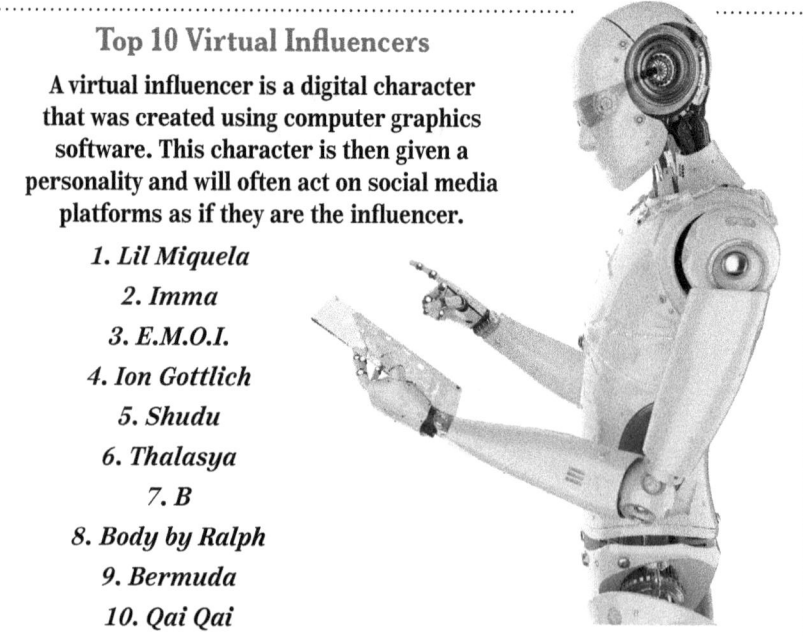

Top 10 Virtual Influencers

A virtual influencer is a digital character that was created using computer graphics software. This character is then given a personality and will often act on social media platforms as if they are the influencer.

1. *Lil Miquela*
2. *Imma*
3. *E.M.O.I.*
4. *Ion Gottlich*
5. *Shudu*
6. *Thalasya*
7. *B*
8. *Body by Ralph*
9. *Bermuda*
10. *Qai Qai*

CONNECT

YOUTUBE

When homework difficulties arise, both parents and kids may feel like elephants in the ocean. But fear not, YouTube has an extensive library of videos to help fledgling scholars.

Whether it's finding the derivative of a logarithmic function, solving a thermodynamic equation, proving a geometry theorem, understanding Shakespeare's King Lear, playing a song on the trumpet, or pronouncing a word in a foreign language, YouTube probably has a video about it. And it's all free (with ads). So whether one's learning something new or reviewing a concept, YouTube's got your back.

Top 10 YouTubers
1. *MrBeast*
2. *PewDiePie*
3. *Like Nastya*
4. *Dude Perfect*
5. *JuegaGerman*
6. *Fernanfloo*
7. *Felipe Neto*
8. *A4*
9. *Bright Side*
10. *Whinderssonnunes*

Source: *Insider*

SPOTIFY

Music without a radio. This global app allows users to create playlists, listen to music and/or podcasts, stream their own work, and share songs with family and friends. The app also has pre-curated playlists of various genres and for various moods. Need help studying? There's a playlist for that. Need music for a birthday party? There's a playlist for that. Need to unwind with a classical Indian raga? There's a playlist for that.

It is worth knowing that Spotify automatically sets your profile and playlists as public, meaning anyone can view them. However, you can adjust this in the app's privacy settings.

FACEBOOK

These days it seems everyone loves or hates Facebook, the social media site on which one can post photos, videos, articles, whereabouts, and comment on other user's posts. But one thing most will agree on is that the platform has had an indelible impact on modern society. In general, Gen Z uses the platform less than their elders, and they're more likely to use it for larger social groups and events. Think school clubs, teams, and seasonal gatherings.

Top 10 Beauty Influencers
1. *Michelle Wong*
2. *Huda Kattan*
3. *Nyane Lebajoa*
4. *Hikari Murakami*
5. *Katie Jane Hughes*
6. *James Charles*
7. *Ashley Quiroz*
8. *Jackie Aina*
9. *Nikkie De Jager*
10. *Nabela Noor*

Source: Influencer Marketing Hub

CONNECT

TWITCH

Not an involuntary muscle movement, nor a nervous tick, but a platform that lets users watch others play video games and/or eSports. Yes, you read that correctly: Twitch lets users watch other people play video games. Think of Twitch as ESPN for eSports and video games.

Because their friends are watching too. And the sofa is comfier than the cold metal bleachers at the football game. And they can still chat with their friends without being drowned out by the announcer. So, mostly because their friends are there.

As for who they watch, the short answer is anyone. Because everybody plays games. Like athletes, gamers vary in their ability, and the best ones inspire others. In fact, video gaming and eSports have become so popular that the International Olympic Committee licensed eSports events, which were held before the formal start of the Tokyo Olympics this past year.

> **Top 9 Twitch Gamers**
> 1. *PewDiePie*
> 2. *Ninja*
> 3. *Shroud*
> 4. *TimTheTatman*
> 5. *Nickmercs*
> 6. *xQc*
> 7. *Syndicate*
> 8. *Summit1g*
> 9. *Pokimane*
>
> Source: Influencer Marketing Hub

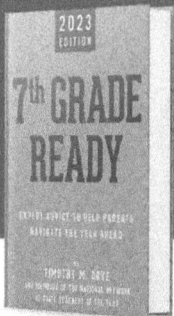

7th Grade Ready

"*7th Grade Ready: Expert Advice for Parents to Navigate the Year Ahead* is a fantastic compilation of advice, strategies, and guidance for how to make it through the year. With special sections on friend groups, executive functioning skills, social and emotional wellness, and how to work with teachers, this handbook is essential for anyone helping a 7th grader."

—**Rebecca Mieliwocki**
2012 National Teacher of the Year

Whether your child is entering middle school for the first time in 7th grade or has already spent a year there as a 6th grader, you'll find loads of information in *7th Grade Ready*. Each contributor is a current or former 7th grade teacher who has worked extensively with parents and families of students and are Teachers of the Year or finalists in their state.

Coming July 2023!

Learn more at **schoolready.guide**

Published by

parentready.com

PLAY
Games

BREAKING DOWN THE WORLD OF VIDEO GAMES

Everybody plays games. From single player to multiplayer modes and from Xbox to gaming PCs, there are a lot of ways for kids to game. Here is a high-level breakdown of the different types of games that your kids might be playing.

VIDEO GAME HARDWARE

Let's start with what your kids might need to get their video game on. Below are four of the most popular hardware consoles for video games.

Xbox: Choose a console depending on your budget and needs—the choices include Series X, Series S, 360, and One. Series X is more powerful and has better resolution but it's also more expensive, and not even necessary for all games. Check what resolution your game is designed in. Overall, Xbox is known for having great graphics, numerous compatible games, and affordability.

PlayStation: Similar to Xbox, PlayStation is known for having superb graphics and a few different consoles to suit your gaming needs. PS5 is the most recent, most powerful edition. Other popular console models include the PS4 Pro and PS4. When it comes to virtual reality, PSVR is a headset that allows gamers an immersive gaming experience.

Gaming PCs: Alienware, Corsair, and Lenovo are all specialized gaming computers, which are great for a serious gamer who wants to invest in hardware that will make their games not only look better, but run much smoother.

Nintendo Switch: Portable and lightweight, the Switch makes gaming possible almost anywhere.

STEAM

Steam is a PC video game distributor that also allows users to create their own games. Starting in 2003 and now boasting over 150 million viewers, the platform has become one of the most popular for kids seeking to escape addled lives. The software is free to download (and can be downloaded onto a regular, non-gaming dedicated desktop), but requires one to pay to play for some games. Beyond price walls, Steam has parental controls called Family View, for which the platform has set-up instructions.

Steam has expansive chat ability, allowing both text and voice chat. Some of the chat forums themselves are public. Still, many kids share their Steam handles with each other so they can play, chat, and trade with their real-life friends online. But beware, it's also possible to do these things with someone your kid doesn't know. A user's default profile setting is public, but as with most social media platforms, this can be adjusted in the user settings.

These are some of the most popular kid-friendly games on Steam:

1. Bloons TD 5
2. Scribblenauts Unlimited
3. Ballistic Mini Golf
4. Minecraft: Story Mode
5. LEGO Star Wars: The Complete Saga

ROBLOX

Roblox is another very popular video gaming platform. Its fastest growing demographic by age is the 17–24 year-old age group. Because games on Roblox are made by its users and there are some purchases made in-game, some gamers have made more than lunch money by monetizing their games. Initially, users earn Robux, Roblox's currency; earn enough Robux and, using Developer Exchange, your kid can earn real money.

Since its inception in 2008, Roblox has paid out $538 million to its community of game developers from around the world. Currently, the site has more than 45 million daily users and a variety of games. Here are some of the most popular games for kids, according to Statista:

1. Adopt Me!
2. Brookhaven
3. Tower of Hell
4. MeepCity
5. Piggy

ESPORTS

eSports are generally referred to as organized, multiplayer video game competitions, which can be between individuals or teams and among professionals or amateurs. The Electronic Sports League supports this type of gaming with various leagues according to game and level. Some leagues include:

ESL Play: includes competitions across a variety of levels.

ESL National Championships: limited by geographic regions, allows qualification to major tournaments.

ESL Pro Tour: continuous tour for professionals only, and currently includes only three Counter-Strike titles: Global Offensive (CS: GO), WarCraft III, and StarCraft III.

> Survey:
> **MAKING FRIENDS**
> 52% of teens report they made a new friend while playing video games last year.

ESL One: offline tournaments for a variety of games, which are often considered some of the most prestigious events for the game as they offer the most prize money.

Other eSports competitions worthy of note:

League of Legends: There's a world championship at stake, worth millions. Players qualify for the world championship through smaller, regional tournaments. Riot Games operates the league.

The International: This is for Dota 2, a multiplayer online battle arena–style game played on Steam. It's an annual competition where millions of dollars are at stake. To qualify, players must receive an invite through the Dota Pro Circuit or regional tournaments.

High School Esports League: Allows high school students the opportunity to compete against each other—sometimes individually and sometimes in teams—in a variety of games from CS: GO and Halo: Infinite to Minecraft and Chess.

North America Scholastic Esports Federation: Offers high school students the chance to compete for eSports scholarships by demonstrating their skills in Rocket League and/or Chess. It's completely free for high school students and runs from the end of September through the end of November.

Other popular eSports games: Fortnite, Hearthstone, Overwatch, Counter-Strike: Global Offensive, League of Legends.

TWITCH

Not only do kids play games, they watch *other people* play games. Why on earth would they want to do this? Because some gamers are better than others and it can be fun to watch your favorite streamers—those who live-stream their video game playing—with friends.

Twitch is where gamers watch other gamers game. It is to the gaming world what ESPN is to real-life sports. Kids can watch anyone game, including some of their peers. British phenom Thomas Simons, better known as his online alias TommyInnit, for example, streams Minecraft. According to TwitchTracker, these are some of the most popular games:

1. Just Chatting
2. League of Legends
3. Grand Theft Auto V
4. VALORANT
5. Counter-Strike: Global Offensive

(See page 39 for the top Twitch games.)

PLAY

In addition to following individual streamers, kids can also watch particular games or gaming platforms. According to TwitchTracker, these are some popular channels:

1. KAICENAT
2. XQC
3. TARIK
4. VALORANT
5. LEC

Blast from the Past: **TOP VIDEO GAMES**

1975
- Breakout
- Pong
- Mattel Auto Race
- Western Gun

1980s
- Jet Set Willy
- Track & Field
- Kung Fu Master
- Out Run
- Robotron 2084
- Gradius
- Pac-Man
- Super Mario Bros. 3
- Tetris

1990s
- Monkey Island
- Gran Turismo
- Resident Evil
- Super Mario Kart
- Street Fighter II
- Sonic the Hedgehog
- Pokémon Red and Blue
- Super Mario 64

2000s
- Marvel vs. Capcom 2: New Age of Heroes
- Twisted Metal: Black
- Final Fantasy X
- Silent Hill 2
- Grand Theft Auto III
- Tony Hawk's Pro Skater 3
- Halo: Combat Evolved
- Crash Bandicoot: The Wrath of Cortex

You Say "Multiverse" & I Say "Metaverse"

In many fictional universes, the "multiverse" refers to the aggregate of all dimensions and parallel realities (or universes) in existence. As Marvel character Doctor Strange said in the 2021 blockbuster *Spider-Man: No Way Home*: "the Multiverse is a concept about which we know frighteningly little."

The "metaverse," in contrast, is perhaps a bit more tangible. It's a big virtual world for us humans here on earth. We can socially interact by giving people a way to make new friends or team up with existing friends in new ways. In 2021, Facebook—now Meta—first showed off its virtual reality metaverse app, *Horizon Worlds*. And the game platforms Roblox and Fortnite moved closer to metaverse status. In the coming year, you will hear a lot about Nvidia's omniverse, which is a platform for creators to build metaverses.

Top Video Games by Genre

ACTION
God of War
Uncharted 4: A Thief's End
Marvel's Spider-Man
Bloodborne
The Last of Us 2

ROLE-PLAYING
The Witcher 3: Wild Hunt
Mass Effect 2
Fallout: New Vegas
Legend of Zelda: Breath of the Wild
Elder Scrolls 5: Skyrim

SPORTS
Rocket League
Lonely Mountains Downhill
Out of the Park Baseball 2023
Tony Hawk's Pro Skater 1 + 2
FIFA 23
Football Manager 2023

MASSIVELY MULTIPLAYER ONLINE
Fortnite
Mario Kart 8: Deluxe
Fall Guys
Call of Duty: Warzone
Sea of Thieves

Source: *gamesradar+*

UNPLUG YOUR KIDS
Recommendations from Toy Store Owner
MICHAEL TIMKO

Plugged-In Parent: When you meet parents, what do you tell them about games?

Michael: Mostly, they are coming into our store for younger kids. And then while they're here, one of the questions we ask them is, do they have siblings? A lot of times, they'll say, "Oh, we have a 12-year-old or 14-year-old but they've grown out of toys."

A lot of these parents say, "I don't know how to get them off of their device." I think the older kids are so plugged into their electronics right now. Every world is at their fingertips, everything is super, super fast. So, when I'm introducing a game that I want a parent or a grandparent to play with their child or grandchild, it's got to be very easy to learn. And very fast to play.

Plugged-In Parent: What kind of games should parents look for that will bring their family together when they have older kids?

Michael: Usually, I try and steer them towards a game that everybody is playing all at the same time. So, there's a race component to it. Not everyone's waiting to take their turn. You're just trying to pull them away from electronics, even if just for two minutes, five minutes, 15 minutes. If you've done that, I feel like you've accomplished a lot.

Some of these games that I recommend could take literally minutes to play an entire game. And if you can unplug them just for that little bit of time, they'll play it over and over and over again.

Plugged-In Parent: So what are these games that you recommend that take minutes to play and everybody's playing at the same time?

Michael: One game I would recommend is called *Tenzi*. It's a dice game and everybody gets their own dice. So you're not sharing dice. And there are eight ways to play and it takes literally minutes to learn each one and to play it. But it's been discovered that there's more than 100 ways to play this game, which means the children or parents can make up their own rules. I've even had teachers buy it for the classroom, pre-COVID of course, where they were using the dice to learn about odd or even numbers, or just pairs. You know, there are different ways you can play. And all it is is dice.

Plugged-In Parent: That's great. And especially the idea that kids can come up with their own versions of the rules. That's amazing.

Michael: Right! And again, it gets them more engaged. They can set a rule that everyone can follow. Because it's that simple to play. The second game that that company came out with—it seems like every year they come out with one game and it's a home run—is called *Slapzi*. It's a card game, where right out of the box, up to eight people can play. It's a fun family game, taking minutes to learn and minutes to play. And it's more social because you have to talk about your answers. It's almost like *Apples-to-Apples*, which is a 12+ game. *Slapzi* is even faster, and everybody is participating all at the same time.

Plugged-In Parent: Are there any other recommendations in that same genre from other manufacturers?

Michael: *Camera Roll*. And the thing about this is that it allows kids to use their device—but all you're using on your device is your camera roll. There are 280 subject cards. You flip over a card while everybody has their device in their hand. The subject might be "something hot." Now you've got to quickly flip through your photos, and share with everybody a picture you took of something that's hot, like a sunset or a fire pit. Or it could even be a selfie. Now your kid is showing everyone this photo and you may ask, "Oh my God, where was that sunset?" Or "Where was that selfie taken?" Now you're creating a dialogue between kids and parents. I've actually had parents discover things about their children that they never even knew because they were actually looking at their photos, not necessarily following them on social media, which might just be a swipe. And you're not totally unplugging the kids as you play. Win-win.

Plugged-In Parent: So you strongly recommend that the parent actually invites their kids to play a game. They shouldn't wait for their kid to come bring something to them?

Michael: Yes, I think the only thing they're going to bring to the parent is their device. And that's not really

---

11 Best Board Games

According to the *New York Times*' Wirecutter

1. *Scythe*
2. *Small World*
3. *Betrayal at House on the Hill*
4. *Mysterium*
5. *Pandemic Legacy: Season 1*
6. *Star Wars: Outer Rim*
7. *Sherlock Holmes Consulting Detective: The Thames Murders and Other Cases*
8. *Cathedral*
9. *Wavelength*
10. *Anomia*
11. *The Quacks of Quedlinburg*

something they're going to experience together as it's more likely a single-player game. I find kids don't share too much with their parents. Their parent might follow them on social media but it's not really being connected with your kids. So yes, I think that the parent needs to introduce something that will unplug them for a few minutes.

MICHAEL TIMKO is founder of Fun Stuff Toys, which is Long Island's premier toy destination and is celebrating its 35th anniversary.

Blast from the Past: **TOP BOARD GAMES**

1975
221b Baker Street
Battle for Germany
Dr. Who
Dungeon!

1980s
Monopoly
Battleship
Operation
Hungry Hungry Hippo
Life
Topple
Trivial Pursuit
Risk
Candy Land
Scrabble

1990s
Settlers of Catan
Magic: The Gathering
Cranium
Twilight Imperium
Atmosfear
Space Crusade
Tigris and Euphrates

2000s
Puerto Rico
Carcassone
Blokus
Scene It?

WATCH
Movies, Series & Specials

Top Streaming Television Series & Movies

We are in the golden age of video streaming. From Netflix and Prime Video to HBOMax and Hulu, there are endless streaming options. Though there is some content crossover between platforms, most tend to offer content produced in-house at the exclusion of content from others. As a result, some parents may feel obligated to subscribe to numerous streaming services. But not all kids are as enthusiastic about television and movies as their parents. According to Deloitte's 2021 Digital Media Trends survey, "only 10% of Gen Z respondents said watching TV or movies was their favorite entertainment pastime," and this preference was fifth among entertainment choices.

That said, for those families who do appreciate a binge-worthy TV show or epic movie, we've compiled lists of greats available across streaming platforms and cable channels this year.

10 TV Series aired in 2022, recommended by *Rotten Tomatoes*:

1. *House of the Dragon* (HBO)
2. *Andor* (Disney+)
3. *Ms. Marvel* (Disney+)
4. *Better Call Saul* (AMC)
5. *Atlanta* (Hulu)
6. *The Bear* (Hulu)
7. *Heartstopper* (Netflix)
8. *Bad Sisters* (AppleTV+)
9. *Hacks* (HBOMAX)
10. *The Boys* (Prime Video)

WATCH

For those who like films designed for the big screen (but can find them on their home TV), here were the most anticipated Summer and Fall 2023 movies, according to *Rotten Tomatoes* (in order of release date):

1. *Spider-Man: Across the Spider-Verse*
2. *Transformers: Rise of the Beasts*
3. *Elemental*
4. *Extraction 2*
5. *The Flash*
6. *Asteroid City*
7. *Indiana Jones and the Dial of Destiny*
8. *Insidious: Fear of the Dark*
9. *Mission Impossible — Dead Reckoning, Part 1*
10. *Roosevelt*
11. *Barbie*
12. *Oppenheimer*
13. *Haunted Mansion*
14. *Meg 2: The Trench*
15. *Teenage Mutant Ninja Turtles: Mutant Mayhem*
16. *Gran Turismo*
17. *Blue Beetle*
18. *The Equalizer 3*
19. *The Nun 2*
20. *Next Goal Wins*
21. *Kraven the Hunter*
22. *The Exorcist*
23. *Pain Hustlers*
24. *Saw X*

If you can't wait for awards season and want a head start on predicting next year's winners, *The Week* has already put together a list of predictions for the Academy Awards 2024. Its Top 10 selections for Best Picture are:

1. *The Holdovers*
2. *Maestro*
3. *Oppenheimer*
4. *Killers of the Flower Moon*
5. *May December*
6. *Ferrari*
7. *Past Lives*
8. *Saltburn*
9. *Next Goal Wins*
10. *Barbie*

TEEN PASSIONS & ACTIONS

Likewise, if you prefer the small screen, *Deadline* has a set of Emmy Awards predictions based on what is slated for release in 2023:

DRAMAS:

1. *Andor* (Disney+)
2. *The Crown* (Netflix)
3. *House of the Dragon* (HBO)
4. *The Last of Us* (HBO)
5. *Lord of the Rings: The Rings of Power* (Amazon Prime Video)
6. *Succession* (HBO)
7. *The White Lotus* (HBO)
8. *Yellowjackets* (Showtime)

COMEDIES:

1. *Abbott Elementary* (ABC)
2. *Barry* (HBO)
3. *The Bear* (FX)
4. *Beef* (Netflix)
5. *The Marvelous Ms. Maisel* (Amazon Prime Video)
6. *Only Murders in the Building* (Hulu)
7. *Ted Lasso* (Apple TV+)
8. *What We Do in the Shadows* (FX)

From Middle Earth and the land of dragons, to a football pitch and a heated kitchen, these shows have a range of settings. There's truly something for everyone, whatever your taste may be.

WHAT TO WATCH ON TV WITH YOUR TEEN

By Eric Deggans

One of the most challenging decisions I might make in a day is what to watch on television.

Not because I'm a TV critic for a national news outlet; figuring out what TV shows NPR listeners might love or should at least find interesting is a fun and adventurous part of a dream job.

But when my 17-year-old son and I are sitting down in front of my new, 65-inch TV, I have one mission: to pick something that will keep him off his phone. For a little bit, at least.

My son, Tobias, is from a generation that has grown up with the convenience of having several screens at his disposal simultaneously. The way he consumes TV shows is vastly different from the strategy deployed by those of us who can remember when the phrase "appointment TV viewing" was more than a quaint concept from media history.

(I still shock some students in my media studies classes when I tell them about how Black folks back in the day would call each other in a telephone tree when they saw a Black person on a TV talk show or variety program. We did it for two reasons: because it was such a rare occurrence and there were few ways to see that moment other than when the network broadcast it.)

These days, when we sit down to decompress in front of the TV, Tobey will pull out his phone and wireless headphones. If I pick a show he finds interesting, he will watch it for a time. But the moment a scene or segment appears that doesn't appeal to him, he'll surf onto YouTube or Tik Tok and find something there that impresses him more.

But he isn't totally checked out of the main event. Instead, he floats back and forth between the two platforms, using his cellphone as an escape hatch whenever the primary TV isn't compelling enough. And what surprises me most in these bits of media gymnastics, is that he doesn't seem to miss much—we will have conversations as the program I'm watching unfolds and he seems to be totally following the action, until I hear a chuckle or a snort, and I realize he's now enjoying a joke on the other platform.

So I have developed a fine eye for what may interest him enough to keep the cellphone watching to a minimum. And it is rarely what you might expect.

WHAT WORKS FOR US

We love, for example, watching old episodes of the TNT drama *The Closer* together. It's a series that starred Kyra Sedgwick as a CIA-trained interrogator brought to head up a task force of experienced Los Angeles police detectives. They work to build cases so strong the perpetrator confesses—usually after an impressively devastating interview with Sedgwick's character.

Two things about this show appeal to us. After the first season, the characters become something of a family, and it is fun to see the ensemble bounce off each other, led by talented actors like J. K. Simmons, G. W. Bailey, and Raymond Cruz. But we're also well aware of how such police procedurals manipulate the audience into rooting for law enforcement to violate people's rights. Officers on *The Closer* routinely trick people into signing away their rights to an attorney or place potential suspects in dangerous situations to pressure confessions.

So part of our ritual in watching *The Closer* is to play "spot the copaganda"—calling out ways in which the officers violate people's rights or tactics the show's producers use to make police excesses seem heroic and necessary.

This is why picking TV shows to watch with Tobey is so challenging. He is a media-savvy teenager, well aware of all the ways modern programming manipulates viewers. Any show which smacks of such techniques or feels in any way contrary to his authentic experience is rejected out of hand.

I rarely bother watching shows with him that are set in high school, for example. He has a fine-tuned ear for clunky dialogue that thirtysomething TV writers put in the mouths of teenage characters, and he's even more perceptive in picking out actors playing teens who probably last saw the inside of a high school ten years ago.

TEEN PASSIONS & ACTIONS

WHAT DOESN'T WORK FOR US

I thought that Netflix's story about the formative years of former NFL star Colin Kaepernick, *Colin in Black & White,* might be an exception. The story depicts Kaepernick's life from eighth grade until his senior year in high school, growing up as the biracial adopted kid of a white couple from Wisconsin who then moved to a mostly-white town in California.

As Kaepernick matured, he reached toward Blackness in ways his parents and friends didn't necessarily understand—wearing his hair in cornrow braids and insisting on taking a Black girl to a formal dance. As a Black father who has raised three biracial kids, including Tobey, I recognize many issues the Netflix series tackles from our own family story—though some of the choices Kaepernick's parents made seemed criminally clueless, even for a white couple from Wisconsin.

I thought Tobey, who is developing his own distinct identity in high school, might also find some things in Kaepernick's story that resonated.

But the episodes are framed by narration from Kaepernick himself, who awkwardly and obviously explains the racial and social dynamics in scenes from his life re-enacted by performers. That tripped Tobey's inauthenticity "Spidey-Sense" and left him cracking jokes about how Netflix had finally made an after-school special "for the kids."

Instead, we enjoy watching cooking competition shows, like Fox's *Hell's Kitchen* and *Masterchef* or *Chopped* on The Food Network—Tobey loves to cook and I love pointing out how reality TV producers manipulate the action. We will watch the best sketches from *Saturday Night Live* on

Sunday morning, recorded on my DVR to make fast forwarding through the clunkers easier.

It's a bit of a double-edged sword to have access to early screeners for new programs through my job as a TV critic. We loved watching Disney+'s *Hamilton* film and episodes of *WandaVision* before many fans had seen them. But when I have to slog through less inspired fare, like Amazon's unscripted show set near our Florida home, *Tampa Baes*, I can pretty much guarantee Tobey will be checked out in cellphone-land (though we did have fun picking out all the places where they actually filmed in our nearby hometown of St. Petersburg and not Tampa).

Blast from the Past: TOP TV SHOWS FOR TEENS

1975
- *Happy Days*
- *The Muppet Show*
- *The Scooby Doo Show*
- *Welcome Back, Kotter*
- *Laverne & Shirley*
- *The Jeffersons*
- *Saturday Night Live*

1980s
- *The Facts of Life*
- *Square Pegs*
- *A Different World*
- *Head of the Class*
- *21 Jump Street*
- *Fame*
- *Growing Pains*
- *Degrassi*
- *Family Ties*

1990s
- *The Fresh Prince of Bel-Air*
- *Boy Meets World*
- *Buffy the Vampire Slayer*
- *Saved by the Bell*
- *Sabrina the Teenage Witch*
- *Beverly Hills, 90210*
- *That '70s Show*
- *Dawson's Creek*
- *Freaks and Geeks*
- *Sister, Sister*
- *Blossom*

2000s
- *Gilmore Girls*
- *One Tree Hill*
- *8 Simple Rules*
- *Malcolm in the Middle*
- *Even Stevens*

TEEN PASSIONS & ACTIONS

A TV CRITIC'S SUGGESTIONS FOR PARENTS

For us, the best TV shows to watch together **inspire conversation**. They also connect us through subjects that we both enjoy or find compelling. I rarely worry about extreme content, but sitting through the ultraviolence of Netflix's *Squid Game* or sexual scenes in some programs can be difficult with my son by my side.

Given that Tobey has access to the wide media world of the Internet, it always seemed counterproductive to try banning him from watching this or that, especially in recent years. Instead, I try to **model good media consumption** myself and encourage him to talk to me about what he's consuming, so I can learn what he's up to and provide guidance, if necessary.

I'm also not above looking over his shoulder every now and then to **keep tabs on what he's watching online**. (As I write this, he is perusing a YouTube channel featuring the Lock Picking Lawyer. Yes, he's an attorney who makes videos on how to pick locks. And he has more than 3.6 million subscribers. I have no idea why.)

To be sure, I'm not one of those parents who blithely accepts whatever their children choose to do. If I thought it was important for Tobey to focus on one thing while we watch TV together, I would take his phone away. But I think it's important to let Tobey **consume media in a way that feels natural to him**, while also offering an option for us to connect in a different way, in a shared media experience that is increasingly old fashioned.

Mostly, I've learned a lot from Tobey about how a younger generation consumes media. Eventually, as kids like him grow up and become more influential consumers, their habits will affect the platforms we all frequent, as media companies strain to stay connected with an audience that multitasks like breathing.

But until then, at least we'll have *The Closer*.

ERIC DEGGANS is NPR's first full-time TV critic.

Blast from the Past: TOP TV SHOWS

1975
All in the Family
Rich Man, Poor Man
Laverne & Shirley
Maude
The Bionic Woman

1980
Dallas
The Dukes of Hazard
60 Minutes
*M*A*S*H*
The Love Boat

1985
The Cosby Show
Family Ties
Murder, She Wrote
60 Minutes
Cheers

1990
Cheers
60 Minutes
Rosanne
A Different World
The Cosby Show

1995
ER
Seinfeld
Friends
Caroline in the City
Monday Night Football

2000
Survivor
ER
Who Wants to Be a Millionaire
Friends
Monday Night Football

HOW TO TALK TO YOUR KIDS ABOUT ZOMBIES...
(& Descendants)
(& also Systemic Inequality)

By Jessica Mason

When we parents were young and tuning into Disney Channel Original Movies, we would occasionally get a kid-friendly lesson about how it was okay to be different or how normal was overrated. It was the standard stuff of kid's entertainment: a gentle moral that left us feeling good. In the years since, media, and the world, have changed a lot and so, of course, have Disney Channel Movies. You may not know it, but a lot of the fluffy musicals your kids are watching on Disney and rewatching endlessly on Disney+ have seriously progressive and important messages about society and inequality. And that's a good thing, because not only do these movies teach really important lessons, they open up important conversations.

So, what are these movies and what do they have to do with social justice?

DESCENDANTS & SYSTEMIC DISENFRANCHISEMENT

If you have a kid between, say, 5 and 15 years old, you have probably heard about Disney's *Descendants* series. There are three movies and a handful of animated shorts and they're all about a world where every Disney movie happened in roughly the same place and time... but it's modern now and all the villains are imprisoned on an island. And all those villains had kids. We follow the children of Maleficent, The Evil Queen, Jafar, and Cruella DeVil as they leave the island and find their place in the lovely, perky world of Auradon, where they learn to be good(ish) and break the chains of toxic parenting. But later in the series everyone, hero and villain alike, learns that systemic disenfranchisement and marginalization leads to radicalization and that real good and progress shouldn't rely on incarceration and punishing children for the sins (real or perceived) of their parents. I mean, there's also stuff about friendship, fitting in, jealousy, and self-actualization too.

The social justice messages in *Descendants* are there but they're subtle. And they mesh with the "villain kid" narrative. Overall, the media trend of re-examining villains is all about re-examining our perceptions and prejudices about people society deems "bad." Vilifying someone as an outsider is way more about keeping one group in power than real danger, and that's an important thing for kids to be thinking about in our increasingly partisan and fractured society.

Z.O.M.B.I.E.S AND SYSTEMIC OPPRESSION

Building off *Descendants*, Disney very clearly wanted to do more when it came to putting social justice on screen with a catchy tune to back it up, which brings us to: *Z.O.M.B.I.E.S*. The official spelling is done that way because the movie is about Zombies who end up cheerleaders. Well, sort of. The story is more complicated than that and, if you look just a bit closer, it's an entire kids' movie musical about systemic oppression, integration, and social justice. Seriously.

Z.O.M.B.I.E.S takes place in the town of Seabrook, where everyone is very normal... except for the Zombies, who are confined in their own area of town (yes, it's a ghetto in the very literal sense). Zombies don't eat brains or hurt people, thanks to wearing something called a "z-band," and so the movie starts with a group of teen zombies joining the human high school. It's very much a sci-fi/kid's horror version of integration of segregated schools, and the Zombies face bad conditions and serious prejudice. Luckily, our two leads, the optimistic Zombie Zed and perky human cheerleader Addison find love. Eventually they show the school and the town that it's okay to be different and that doesn't mean Zombies need to conform to the white(bread) existence of Seabrook.

This movie is pretty explicitly about social justice. Characters frankly discuss if they should change to fit the overculture; and their differences are exploited when convenient while they are still being marginalized. People learn to overcome prejudice, but not everyone overcomes it entirely. And it's all set to some great pop music. Both the movie and the music are influenced a lot by *Hamilton*, from the pop and rap synthesis to the most social progressive character being named Eliza.

WATCH

Z.O.M.B.I.E.S 2 AND SOCIAL JUSTICE

The ideas of justice are even louder in the sequel, wherein it's revealed that the settlers of Seabrook stole a magical power source from the indigenous people there and now they want it back. Those people are werewolves, yes, but the story about returning indigenous resources and how everyone, even marginalized groups like the Zombies, can take part in oppressive systems is important and powerful. Of course, it ends in an inspiring and hopeful way, but it's frankly incredible to see a movie made for kids take on issues this complex and do it in such an entertaining and nuanced way. There's a third *Zombies* film on the way in 2022 that will involve aliens, and if it takes on immigration and refugees, I won't be shocked.

> **Blast from the Past:**
> **BEST HORROR MOVIES**
> *Carrie* (1976)
> *The Funhouse* (1981)
> *Nightmare on Elm Street* (1985)
> *It* (1990)
> *The Return of the Texas Chainsaw Massacre* (1995)
> *Final Destination* (2000)

FINDING REPRESENTATION

The casts of these films are diverse and the music itself draws from all sorts of sources, so not only are these movies exposing kids to all sorts of ideas, but also allowing *everyone* to see themselves on screen. One thing I would like to see more of in these kinds of movies going forward is more explicit queer representation. While *Descendants* and *Zombies* have several characters we can easily interpret as LGBTQ, it's not textual and that's something YA media needs more of—and has in an increasing number of kids' series, including Disney series like *The Owl House* and *Andi Mack*.

TEEN PASSIONS & ACTIONS

These movies don't just work because they're full of great dancing, fun music, and memorable characters; they're special because they allude to, or directly address, issues that are incredibly important right now in America, and in the lives of the kids watching them. But they use fantasy to make them accessible. And that's why it's important for us, as parents, to be aware of this, because these are important conversations to have. When you can reference something that your child already knows when discussing something important in the news, that makes the conversation that much easier.

JESSICA MASON is an author, podcaster, and fangirl based in Portland, Oregon, where she lives with her wife, daughter, and corgi.

Best Scary Movies for Teens (rated PG or PG-13)

Arachnophobia (1990)
Poltergeist (2015)
Something Wicked This Way Comes (1983)
Scary Stories to Tell in the Dark (2019)
A Quiet Place (2018)
Happy Death Day (2017)
The Sixth Sense (1999)
The Watcher in the Woods (1980)
Signs (2002)
The Ring (2002)
The Village (2004)
Lady in the Water (2006)
The Birds (1963)
The Others (2001)
Super 8 (2011)

Why Kids Like to Be Scared

According to psychologist David Rudd, people enjoy being scared because deep down they know they aren't in real danger, making the experience exciting rather than truly frightening.

Most adults and teenagers are able to gauge the actual threat that scary stimuli pose to them, meaning they understand that there is no physical threat to their safety and can enjoy the sensation of fear.

Younger children, however, cannot correctly gauge the risk posed to them by scary stimuli, meaning they believe they are in real danger and experience real fear. This is why children usually don't enjoy scary activities (horror movies, haunted houses, etc.) until their brains develop as teenagers.

We are in the midst of a "Teen Mental Health Crisis"

Navigating Teen Mental Health: An Expert's Guide for Parents provides step-by-step guidance so parents can confidently and effectively support their children. Child and adolescent clinical psychologist Dr. Tyish Hall Brown answers parents' toughest questions and provides talking points to jumpstart difficult conversations with confidence.

Learn more at **teenmentalhealth.guide**

Published by
PARENT READY
parentready.com

Top 10 Scary Roller Coasters

1. Top Thrill Dragster
Cedar Point, Sandusky, OH
- 420 feet tall
- Reaches 120 mph

2. Kingda Ka
Six Flags Great Adventure, Jackson, NJ
- 456 feet tall—tallest roller coaster in the world
- Top speed 128 mph—fastest coaster in North America
- Goes from 0 to 128 mph in 3.5 seconds—90 degrees straight up
- Ends with 129-foot camel hump

3. X2
Six Flags Magic Mountain, Valencia, CA
- 200 feet tall
- Top speed 76 mph
- 360-degree rotating seats
- Drops face-down
- Two "raven turns"—half loops that turn into sheer drops

4. Superman: Escape from Krypton
Six Flags Magic Mountain, Valencia, CA
- 415 feet high
- Goes from 0 to 100 mph in 7 seconds—in reverse
- Launches 90 degrees upward to 415 feet
- Experience weightlessness for 6.5 seconds
- Falls back down at 92 mph

5. Intimidator 305
Kings Dominion, Doswell, VA
- 305 feet tall
- First drop is 300 feet at 85-degree angle

6. Valravn
Cedar Point, Sandusky, OH
- 223 feet tall
- 90-degree drop
- 270-degree roll

7. SheiKra
Busch Gardens, Tampa, FL
- Reaches 75 mph
- 90-degree drop
- Splash landing

8. Griffon
Busch Gardens, Williamsburg, VA
- Reaches 75 mph
- 90-degree drop

9. El Toro
Six Flags Great Adventure, Jackson, NJ
- Wooden roller coaster
- Reaches 70 mph
- Steepest drop of any wooden roller coaster in the U.S.

10. Fury 325
Carowinds, Charlotte, NC
- 325 feet tall
- Reaches 95 mph
- 81-degree steepness
- World's tallest, fastest, longest giga coaster

READ
YA Franchises & Fan Fiction

Top Young Adult Franchises & Novels

Thankfully, Gen Z still reads books, especially young adult novels. For those who are unfamiliar with this genre, its defining characteristic is that it's marketed towards a tween and teenage audience. Typically, these books also include a protagonist around middle or high school age, the same age as most readers, and have themes about growing up, losing innocence, finding themselves in a bigger world, etc. A few sub-genres include fantasy, sci-fi, romance, and coming-of-age. When it comes to describing Gen Z's taste in young adult novels, **diversity** is the buzzword. Gen Zers want books with relatable characters, regardless of who wrote or published the work. Gen Z is more likely to buy books on Amazon but they'll go to their local bookstore if they're lucky enough to live near one. Because there are more options for publishing these days, there's also more content. We've compiled a list of lists, from franchises we think your kids will discover and love to lesser-known young adult novels published this year, to all-time greats for everyone to enjoy, regardless of age. These lists are not exhaustive, merely a good place to start.

READ

Franchises with enduring power most kids will discover:

1. *Harry Potter* by J. K. Rowling
2. *Percy Jackson & The Olympians* by Rick Riordan
3. *The Hunger Games* by Suzanne Collins
4. *The Lord of the Rings* by J. R. R. Tolkein
5. *Divergent* by Veronica Roth
6. *The Maze Runner* by James Dashner
7. *Twilight* by Stephanie Meyer
8. *Alex Rider* by Anthony Horowitz
9. *Diary of a Wimpy Kid* by Greg Heffley
10. *The Chronicles of Narnia* by C. S. Lewis
11. *His Dark Materials* by Philip Pullman
12. *Pretty Little Liars* by Sara Shepard
13. *The Hitchhiker's Guide to the Galaxy* by Douglas Adams
14. *The Wrinkle in Time Quintet* by Madeline L'Engle
15. *The Giver Quartet* by Lois Lowry
16. *Bone* by Jeff Smith

Fall usually marks the start of a new school year, and most kids would like a break from their schoolwork. Consider adding to their shelves something from this list of Summer 2023 titles by *Buzzfeed*. These books take place in various settings and include protagonists from a range of backgrounds.

1. *An Appetite for Miracles* by Laekan Zea Kemp
2. *Ander and Santi Were Here* by Jonny Garza Villa
3. *Bianca Torre is Afraid of Everything* by Justine Pucella Winans
4. *The Song of Wrath* by Sarah Raughley
5. *That Self-Same Metal* by Brittany N. Williams
6. *Warrior Girl Unearthed* by Angeline Boulley
7. *Lying in the Deep* by Diana Urban
8. *Venom & Vow* by Anna-Marie McLemore & Elliott McLemore

TEEN PASSIONS & ACTIONS

9. *Her Good Side* by Rebekah Weatherspoon
10. *Ride or Die* by Gail-Agnes Musikavanhu
11. *Everyone Wants to Know* by Kelly Loy Gilbert
12. *Sing Me to Sleep* by Gabi Burton
13. *A Song of Salvation* by Alechia Dow
14. *Their Vicious Games* by Joelle Wellington
15. *Guardians of Dawn: Zhara* by S. Jae-Jones

When kids grow tired of their old picture books, and perhaps reading in general, it need not be difficult for kids—or their parents—to replace them. The American Library Association recommends these ten books for reluctant readers:

1. *Be Not Far from Me* by Mindy McGinnis
2. *Found* by Joseph Bruchac
3. *Golden Arm* by Carl Deuker
4. *Heartstopper Vol. 1* by Alice Oseman
5. *Long Way Down: The Graphic Novel* by Jason Reynolds and Danica Novgorodoff
6. *The Loop* by Ben Oliver
7. *#NoEscape* by Gretchen McNeil
8. *Punching the Air* by Ibi Zoboi and Yusef Salaam
9. *Snapdragon* by Kat Leyh
10. *You Should See Me in a Crown* by Leah Johnson

Are you (or your kids) looking for something to read over the summer holiday or during winter break? According to Bustle, the following 17 titles, all published in the 21st century, are also great reads:

1. *Aristotle and Dante Discover the Secrets of the Universe* by Benjamin Alire Sáenz
2. *The Absolutely True Diary of a Part-Time Indian* by Sherman Alexie
3. *Empress of a Thousand Skies* by Rhoda Belleza
4. *The Hate U Give* by Angie Thomas
5. *Feathers* by Jacqueline Woodson

READ

6. *Love Is the Drug* by Alaya Dawn Johnson
7. *Done Dirt Cheap* by Sarah Nicole Lemon
8. *Out of Darkness* by Ashley Hope Pérez
9. *The Coldest Girl in Coldtown* by Holly Black
10. *Lair of Dreams* by Libba Bray
11. *Iron Cast* by Destiny Soria
12. *The Sun is Also a Star* by Nicola Yoon
13. *Yaqui Delgado Wants to Kick Your Ass* by Meg Medina
14. *Witch Eyes* by Scott Tracey
15. *Pointe* by Brandy Colbert
16. *American Street* by Ibi Zoboi
17. *Sacrifice* by Cindy Pon

Books make great birthday presents for those who love to read. Consider giving your kid one of these ten books that have appeared on all-time great young adult reads, but are not included in any of the lists above:

1. *Stargirl* by Jerry Spinelli
2. *The Fault in Our Stars* by John Green
3. *The Book Thief* by Markus Zusak
4. *The Perks of Being a Wallflower* by Stephen Chbosky
5. *The Outsiders* by S. E. Hinton
6. *Holes* by Louis Sachar
7. *The House on Mango Street* by Sandra Cisneros
8. *Animal Farm* by George Orwell
9. *To Kill a Mockingbird* by Harper Lee
10. *Fahrenheit 451* by Ray Bradbury

A PARENT'S GUIDE TO FAN FICTION

By Jessica Mason

If your teen or tween spends time online in fandom, chances are, they're reading fan fiction, better known as fanfic, and that can be a great thing… or a scary thing. Or both! Just like fic! So, let's break down what fanfic is, where kids tend to find it, and how you can be proactive in talking to your kid about some of the wilder things they may encounter.

WHAT IS FANFIC?

Fan fiction is very much what it sounds like: fiction written by fans of a certain story or franchise, essentially taking the characters someone else created and telling a new tale. Did you ever see a movie or read a book and loved it all the way up until the ending when the wrong person died, or the wrong couple got a happily ever after, so you wrote your own version where it ended the *right* way? That's fanfic.

Fanfic is what the smarty pants academics and lawyers call **transformative work**, meaning it takes source material and transforms it. When you think about it in that way, a lot of things are actually fanfic. James Joyce's *Ulysses* is fanfic of Homer's *Odyssey*; *House* is *Sherlock Holmes* fanfic. *Thor* is fanfic of Norse mythology, and even *Hamilton* is fanfic of the revolutionary war.

READ

Writing and consuming fanfic is one of the primary activities that teens (and adults) partake in when they are active in *fandom*. Fandom, if you don't know by now, goes beyond just liking a show, movie, or book series. It involves *interacting* with that content in a sustained and substantial way. For instance, I don't just love *Supernatural*, I look for posts about it on social media and make my own. I care about romantic partnerships in the show, and I read and write fanfic based on it. I'm in the fandom. Contrast that to a show like *Game of Thrones*, where I'll watch it and enjoy it, but I won't go deeper than that.

WHY FANFIC?

Fanfic happens because fans really care about and get attached to characters in their media. They want more stories, and in many instances, they want to get something that the primary source (what fans call *canon*) isn't giving them. This can be a new or alternative story set in the same world as the original, or a fanfic can take the characters and put them in a different world. We call that ***alternative universe***, or ***AU***.

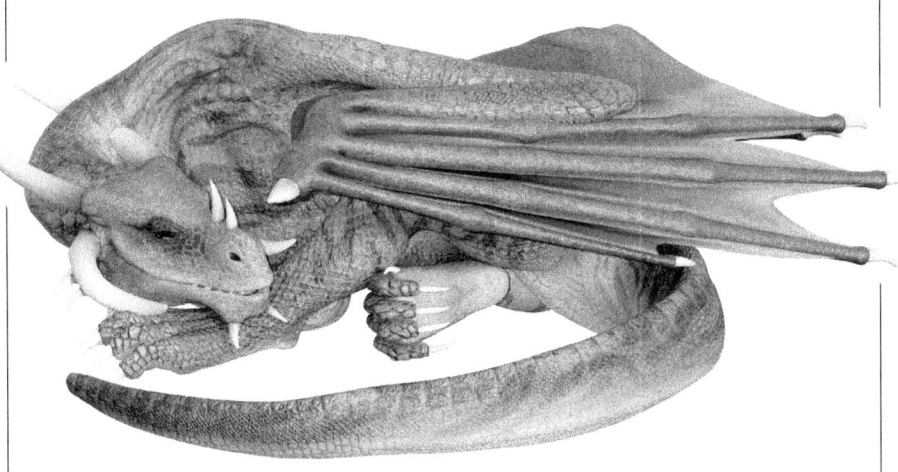

What kind of stories do you get in fanfic? All of them! It can be anything, but most of the time what fans want from fic is romance, that is, specific romances between certain characters. Fanfic is a big part of **shipping**, which we define as actively rooting for two people to get together in a romantic relation*ship*.

Why is your teen interacting with strangers on Twitter? Why are they writing manifestos to the CW? Nine out ten times, it's a shipping thing. The best way to enjoy a ship, however, is to read a few hundred stories in which your preferred pair (or polycule) gets together for a happy ending. Now, not all fanfic is romantic, but a lot of it is, and that's where this can get tricky for parents.

MATURE THEMES

Fanfic in many ways is the free internet equivalent of a romance novel, with all the steamy content that can entail. There is lots of fanfic out there, and much of it is very explicit. It also can include all manner of spiciness, from kink to tentacles to a whole genre of fanfic devoted to mating and heat cycles akin to canines. And a lot, if not the majority, of fanfic is what's called **slash**, meaning it's about a romantic/sexual relationship between two men. You'll see fanfic about queer women as well, but it's probably the third most common type of fanfic behind slash and heterosexual pairings.

What you need to know, as a parent, is that a lot of explicit fanfic is easily available online. The most popular fanfic platforms are websites, including fanfiction.net, Wattpadd, and the most well-known, Archive of Our Own, or AO3. I recommend you explore these sites to be familiar with them. AO3 specifically operates under a policy that it doesn't police or censor any sort of fic, but it is expected that authors use both **ratings** and **tags**.

Just like movie ratings, the ratings on AO3 reflect a broad spectrum of maturity. There's G for general audiences and, T for teen, M for mature, and E for explicit. Further, fics should have tags that reflect if there is violence, rape, major character death, or other things, from cuddling to BDSM. There's a tag for everything—and it's not just a tool for people to filter fic they don't want to read but also to find things that they specifically like. There are internet content filters out there that can block sites like AO3, but to be honest, if your kid is into a fandom and internet-savvy enough to look for fic, they can probably get around those. AO3 will give unregistered users a prompt telling them, "This work could have adult content. If you proceed you have agreed that you are willing to see such content." But again, that probably won't stop the committed or curious.

WHAT PARENTS SHOULD KNOW AND DO

I wouldn't let a tween on sites like AO3 until they are mature enough, but use your judgement for teens. If they're not ready for a trashy paperback, they should be careful around fanfic. But fanfic is also the way a lot of youngsters first discover this kind of content and explore their sexuality. The use of characters they know creates a safe space to see what kind of things and people they like. Especially for LGBTQ kids, it's important for them to have outlets when the media isn't giving them a variety of representation. And it's also the first thing many teens write, and it's a great way to hone literary skills.

I don't recommend searching your child's AO3 reading history, as that would be a pretty big violation of privacy. But if your kid is reading fanfic, it's probably a good idea to have some frank talk about safe sex, consent, and reality versus fiction. A lot of fic endeavors to portray safer sex practices like condom use, and much of the kinkier stuff is far better at discussing boundaries and consent than even your typical bodice ripper. But, it's not *all* good and so you might want to have some talks with your teen if you see them on AO3 or another site. Make sure they know that this is still fiction and in the real world, not every encounter is going to have a happy ending.

JESSICA MASON is an author, podcaster, and fangirl based in Portland, Oregon where she lives with her wife, daughter, and corgi.

READ

Blast from the Past: **BEST TEEN BOOKS**

1975

The Grey King
by Susan Cooper

The Great Ghost Rescue
by Eva Ibbotson

Tuck Everlasting
by Natalie Babbit

Eight Days of Luke
by Diana Wynne Jones

1980

The Magicians of Caprona
by Diana Wynne Jones

Space Patrol
by Steven Caldwell

The Fantastic Planet
by Steven Caldwell

Voorloper
by Andre Norton

1985

Talking to Dragons
by Patricia C. Wrede

Deep Wizardry
by Diane Duane

Tailchaser's Song
by Tad Williams

A Hidden Magic
by Vivian Vande Velde

1990s

Harry Potter Books 1-3
by J.K. Rowling

The Giver
by Lois Lowry

The Perks of Being a Wallflower
by Stephen Chbosky

Monster
by Walter Dean Myers

Tuck Everlasting
by Natalie Babbitt

Both Sides of Time
by Caroline B. Cooney

2000

Paper Towns
by John Green

The Twilight Saga
by Stephenie Meyer

The Hunger Games
by Suzanne Collins

Looking for Alaska
by John Green

Simon vs. the Homo Sapiens Agenda
by Becky Albertalli

Fangirl by Rainbow Rowell

Thirteen Reasons Why
by Jay Asher

ANIME & MANGA: THROUGH THE LENS OF OUR CHILDREN

By Tracey Jai Pannell

The developmental years are inarguably important, as these are the impressionable moments that shape our kids' futures. Being molded by the environment around them, the content they watch should be educational, instilling them with beneficial lessons that are applicable to their lives. As the internet continues expanding, there's an increasing amount of negativity that can be harmful to malleable minds. It's crucial for our kids to have positive influences, including people they can look up to other than parents and teachers. Their surroundings should provide guidance through these hormonal, angsty times.

Imagination is at the forefront of our childhood experience. It's a healthy form of escapism, giving us a break from the real world. Anime and manga give our kids the opportunity to delve into a fantasyland filled with adventure and meaningful experiences. Originating in Japan, these stories illustrate inspiring, dauntless characters and their journeys through life. At first glance, it may be hard to understand why our kids are interested in anime and manga. From an outsider's perspective, there's often a negative connotation with the subculture due to misinformation. Unbeknownst to many, manga's roots are intertwined deeply with America. According to Fleischer Studios, the creators of Betty Boop, Osamu Tezuka's inspiration for *AstroBoy,* the first manga, is attributed to Betty's character design. Without the creation of her, manga and anime wouldn't exist as we know it today.

CHARACTERS AS ROLE MODELS

These characters turn into role models for our children, giving them someone to admire and be entertained by. Some popular titles you might've heard of are: *Naruto*, *Yu-Gi-Oh!*, *Splatoon*, *Bakugan Battle Brawlers*, *Pokémon*, and *Sonic the Hedgehog*. These stories depict characters that are heroic, compassionate, and industrious. They are faced with seemingly inconceivable problems yet are able to persevere using sheer will and motivation. The life lessons displayed by storytelling give insight to realistic situations and how to handle them responsibly.

Naruto reflects a coming-of-age story of a boy who was put through numerous predicaments. Naruto Uzumaki is able to stay determined. In spite of everything pitted against him, his personality is consistently energetic and lighthearted. Ash Ketchum from *Pokémon* is altruistic, helping anyone in need he comes across, including Pokémon. During Pokémon battles, now and then, he'll make mistakes and lose. After all, he's only a young boy exploring the world around him.

These are just two of many characters that demonstrate affirmative beliefs of benevolence and fortitude. Messages like this teach our kids the importance of improvement and growth, showing them not to succumb to life's hardballs. Instead, they can turn these situations into teaching moments.

A CREATIVE INFLUENCE

The emerging teenage years transpire into a stage of experimentation with identity and this can be shown through personal style and hobbies. An article from *The Guardian* discusses how manga is increasingly becoming an influence for young writers. Three established female writers from Great Britain have attributed their successes to the inspiration gained through reading manga and comic books.

Mangas are similar to comics, but are read from right to left, meaning the first page starts in the back.

An interest in anime and manga can overlap with other creative outlets, like drawing and fashion. Sanrio characters from Japan like Hello Kitty have made their mark in high fashion, even being seen on the runway. Anime's influence has seeped into a multitude of mediums; even popular music artists pay homage to the subculture. Japanese culture has always been of interest to Americans; its unique components contribute to the appeal.

GUIDELINES FOR PARENTS

Some believe that all anime and mangas are marketed to children, though this is not the case. They can be geared towards older teenage audiences and there is also content out there for adults only. For example, *Dragon Ball Z*, *One Punch Man*, *Hunter x Hunter*, and *One Piece* depict some scary violent scenes that may not be appropriate for an emerging teen. Be aware of what titles your children watch and read; do your own research to determine what you deem suitable. Some recommended anime for family bonding include *Little Witch Academia*, *Yo-kai Watch*, and *Sailor Moon*.

15 Best Anime Series for Beginners

One Punch Man
Naruto
Fullmetal Alchemist: Brotherhood
Attack on Titan
Cowboy Bebop
Dragon Ball
Pokémon
Sword Art Online
One Piece
Samurai Champloo
Demon Slayer: Kimestu no Yaiba
Yuri on Ice
Erased
My Hero Academia
Parasyte

Source: Japan Web Magazine

TEEN PASSIONS & ACTIONS

Studio Ghibli Films, although animated in Japan, are not technically considered anime. However, these movies are a great way to hang out and familiarize yourself with the topic. They differ mainly because of the animation style and storytelling. These heartwarming movies are about perseverance, family, and friendship. Audiences of all ages watch these films. Suggested Studio Ghibli Films to enjoy are *My Neighbor Totoro*, *Spirited Away*, *Ponyo*, and *Kiki's Delivery Service*.

Japanese animation and books have left a lasting impression on our youth. Appealing to various walks of life, it gives them a chance to take a needed break from the world. It allows them to explore a multifarious universe, filled with meritorious characters. It opens the door for discussions about the meaning of loyalty, goals, friendship, love, respect, and determination. By relaying the tools necessary to be well-rounded and good-natured, anime and manga emboldens our children. It promotes creative thought and individuality that carries throughout their lifetimes.

TRACEY JAI PANNELL has a B.B.A specializing in visual fashion; her artwork is on display at numerous exhibitions.

CONNECTING WITH YOUR KIDS THROUGH COMIC BOOKS

An Interview with FRANK CARUSO

Frank Caruso is a cartoonist and author who has collaborated with Bruce Springsteen, Andrew Vachss, and Green Day. He is also Betty Boop's creative director. Therefore we thought he'd be the perfect man to talk to about how to connect with our kids through comic books and graphic novels.

Plugged-In Parent: As somebody who's managed comic books, as a consumer of comic books, and as a dad of comic book fans, what do you think parents need to know about comic books today?

Frank: Comic books today definitely deal a lot with, as in the past, superheroes and fighting evil forces. But what parents should know is they also deal with social issues and are more reality-based than fantasy-based. There are plenty of comic books out there in which no one's wearing a cape or a mask; they're dealing with real-life issues, whether

it's bullying, drugs or—any social issues that kids deal with. So it's important for parents to know that it's not just fantasyland anymore. Comic books are dealing with issues that parents should be aware of.

And these past 20 years of superhero movies shows that comics are not just a kid's medium anymore. Everyone understands the stories and the depth of the storylines. So comics are something, more than ever, that parents and kids *together* can relate to. Imagine how cool I felt when my daughter was impressed that I mentioned the Southside Serpents while she was watching an episode of *Riverdale*. She said, "Dad! how do you know these characters?!" I said, "Because I read Archie Comics as a kid!"

Plugged-In Parent: Let's say as a comic book fan of the past, how can parents use comic books as a way to connect with their tween kids, aged 11 to 13?

Frank: Well, one of the things is, like I said, they deal with social issues. One that I was personally involved with, *Heart Transplant* (Darkhorse Books), dealt with the topic of bullying because, unfortunately, it's an issue that runs rampant in every school. My partner and co-author Andrew Vachss wrote *Heart Transplant* as a graphic novel and I illustrated it with the same intensity as Andrew's words as to underscore the severity of the bullying crisis that kids see every day in school. The overall concept was to make the novel creatively appealing to both kids *and* parents. With razor-sharp writing and art that ranged from pencil sketches to paintings, Andrew and I achieved our goal of having the book open the lines of communication between parents and their kids and be a starting point to discuss the topic. We also worked hard to get *Heart Transplant* donated to school libraries.

Plugged-In Parent: And so, where does a parent go nowadays if they want to start a conversation about a social issue? Where do they go to buy a comic if their hometown doesn't have a comic bookstore anymore?

Frank: Just go right to Amazon, or Google it online. You could even type in a topic, such as graphic novels about bullying or drug abuse, and believe me, there's going to be a whole series out there. If your kids are interested in a certain fantasy genre anime, or what they watch on TV or online, chances are, there's

---

Blast from the Past: **TOP COMIC BOOK FRANCHISES**

1975
The Amazing Spider-Man
Giant Size Man-Thing
Fantastic Four
Thor
Conan the Barbarian
X-Men
Superman
The Avengers

1980s
Akira
The Dark Knight Returns
Watchmen
Teenage Mutant Ninja Turtles
Crisis on Infinite Earths

1990s
Batman: Knightfall
Daredevil
The Sandman
Preacher
Deadpool
Kingdom Come
Bone
The Infinity War
Sin City
Hellboy
X-Men: Age of Apocalypse
The Death and Return of Superman

2000s
Spider-Man Obama Issue
Civil War
The Dark Knight Strikes Again
X-Men
Spawn

TEEN PASSIONS & ACTIONS

going to be a crossover comic and you could recommend it. And parents can be more involved with the subject matter that their kids are reading.

Plugged-In Parent: It used to be that parents and kids could bond over the weekday or Sunday comics. What do you see going on in newspaper comics that parents should know about; is that a reason they should subscribe to the newspaper again?

Frank: It's funny because I'm a huge fan of that world, and spent a lot of my career in it. Unfortunately, it's not what it used to be. A cartoonist once called the newspaper comic strip the great American art form, comic strips *and* jazz [laughs]. But newspapers are declining and everyone's reading everything online. You can pretty much get any comic you want online. Whereas in the old days you bought the newspaper every day and statistics showed that after the front page, the comics page was the next section everyone went to because it was like visiting an old friend. Whether it was the old ones, like *Beetle Bailey, Blondie, Flash Gordon*, or the serial superhero ones, like *The Phantom*, or modern-day ones, like *Zits* or *Baby Blues*, that deal with home life. *Dennis the Menace*. I don't know that kids today are reading newspaper comic strips. I would say your youngest demographic for newspaper comics are in their upper thirties, if not forties, guys buying the paper for the sports section. Cartoonists of the newspaper world are trying to adapt to the digital world and getting work online. But there's a lot of competition. In the old days, you could squeeze in maybe 10 or 12 strips on one newspaper page. And that was it. Like the old days of television, there were three or four networks, and everyone watched those shows. Now, there are a thousand networks and streaming services. So there's a lot out there to read and I just don't see

READ

younger kids going out there to read a comic strip like *Hagar the Horrible* or *Dennis the Menace* anymore.

Plugged-In Parent: I had never heard that the comic strip is the great American art form. Can you elaborate on that?

Frank: Keep in mind that's coming from a cartoonist. If you go back to the early days of Pulitzer and Hearst, that phrase "yellow journalism" really came around because of comic strips. They were battling each other in the newspaper wars at the turn of the century. Hearst had one cartoonist and Pulitzer was trying to steal that cartoonist because the comics were attracting the readers. And then Pulitzer added red to one of his comics, adding color to the pages for the first time, and then Hearst put yellow on a strip called *The Yellow Kid*. And that's where the phrase yellow journalism came from because they were really slinging it back and forth, fighting it out over cartoonists, because that was attracting people to their papers.

Plugged-In Parent: Last question: If a parent has an aspiring animator, or cartoonist, what advice would you give them?

Frank: Well, animation and comics are two different worlds. But I speak with a lot of young people, friends with kids that want to go to art school, or they love comic books or animation. The advice I give them is to always encourage them to draw, encourage them to read because reading is a part of it. And that's where comic books help, coming back to your first question: to get them to read the comic books about what interests them. And kids like to write their own, which is something that's important, and it's not bad to start doing it online. When we were kids, we did it for our friends, we used to draw and staple them together and give them out to our friends in school. Now you can do it online. And you can even animate online—there

are simple programs that kids can do. And it really makes them feel like they're creating, especially when their friends can see it because, bottom line is, you're trying to make people laugh, or tugging at the heartstrings, or trying to get something you believe in across. So support them to keep drawing, learn the tools, go digital. If you're drawing on pen and paper, that's great, I still do it, but you have to buy your Wacom pad and start drawing digitally and coloring, learn the programs, and just have fun with it. Encourage the kids; that's what my parents did. They were schoolteachers, they didn't know much about the art world, but they introduced me to the art teachers in their schools. My mom's friends, the English teachers, all wanted to write children's books—how many books I illustrated when I was a kid, just to help them out. But I loved doing it. Bottom line is you have to love doing it. So, encourage them, learn about it, give them some of the tools to play around with, and just tons to look at. Something's going to strike home with them. Something's going to register.

Plugged-In Parent: That's great. Anything else you want to add?

Frank: The big takeaway is about communication, having parents and kids opening the lines of communication, especially with graphic novels. Even go back and read some of the old ones. When I was in art school, one of my teachers was Art Spiegelman, and he was working on *Maus*. He had interviewed his father. If kids don't like history, they're going to read *Maus* and they're going to learn about the Holocaust and in a form that kids not only relate to but enjoy. And to this day, *Maus* is the only graphic novel to win a Pulitzer Prize.

Plugged-In Parent Summer Challenge

Reconnect with the passions of your kids with this 12-week challenge! Meant to encourage you, as parents, to show your kids that you're actively interested in them and their interests with an element of fun for both of you and an element of adventure, allowing for spontaneous eruption of conversation, taking each of you out of your comfort zone.

Start this 12-week challenge once your kid has finished school. Pick one activity from these six categories each week, depending on the interests of your kid. Or make one up on your own!

1. cook
2. move
3. create
4. play/share
5. give back
6. Go!

Cook

- Shop for and cook a meal together from a recipe that your kid chooses.

- Bake 24 cookies together—eat 12 and encourage your kid to give the rest to friends.

- Do a tasting with samples from all of your kid's favorite fast-food joints.

- Host your own pizza night. Buy premade dough, let your kid and their friends roll it out and add their own toppings.

- Plan a taco Tuesday party. Ask your kid to help prep all the various ingredients and toppings and invite their friends.

- Invite some friends over for an ice cream sundae bar.

CONNECT

Move

- Get the family together to play your kid's favorite sport.
- Work out with your child to their exercise routine.
- Go for a sunset bike ride.
- Take a nighttime swim in a pool or ocean.
- Set up some chalkboard games like shuffleboard or four-square and have a tournament.
- Set up a neighborhood scavenger hunt and make it a race.

Create

- Look through a photo album and research a family tree together.
- Ask your kid to reimagine their bedroom.
- Make a memory box from the highlights of a recent trip.
- Host a photo shoot starring your child at a beautiful location, or give them a list of 10 things to shoot and present in a slide show.

- Let your child help you redo your wardrobe or pick your nail color for the week.
- Create an outdoor party with lights and decorations—let your child pick the theme.

TEEN PASSIONS & ACTIONS

Play/Share

- Play a board or card game your kid selects.
- Play a video of game of your kid's choosing.
- Read a book that your child read during the school year and talk about it, or pick a book for the upcoming school year to read together and discuss.
- Start a short story with your child, each writing a paragraph or page every day of that week.
- Have your child pick a movie and set up an outdoor screening.
- Ask to watch a few of your kid's favorite YouTube/TikTok videos. Ask them what they would talk about if they made their own video.

Give Back

- Help a neighbor together, whether it's mowing a lawn or going grocery shopping.
- Pitch in with a local cleanup (i.e., beach, park, or hiking path).
- Spend a day with a local food delivery service for impaired or elderly residents.
- Offer a neighborhood car wash and donate the profits.
- Spend a day at a local community garden.
- Set up a lemonade/baked goods stand and donate any profits.

CONNECT

Go!

- Ask your kid to name a few things they'd like to see on a hike and pick appropriately.
- Walk to your kid's favorite treat shop (i.e., ice cream, favorite bakery).
- Let your teen drive a golf cart.
- Go on a graffiti crawl.
- Start a fire together (somewhere safe and appropriate).
- Camp out in your backyard—complete with tents and s'mores.

LISTEN
Music

UNDERSTANDING TODAY'S POP MUSIC

By Noah Caruso

Today's hits. Bubblegum music. Top 40. Call it whatever you'd like, pop music is recurrent in the musical landscape, and something that seems to change across each generation. Though the sounds and scenes of pop music appear to be vastly different from what they were before, the reality is that the formula is still the same. The music industry targets pop music toward the youth of each generation, just as it did 40 years ago. Rest assured, understanding what your kid is listening to—and why—isn't as hard as it may seem.

I'll repeat: pop music is directed towards the youth. Sorry, parents, but new and young is in. And, like anything, the music industry is a business. So when these two things collide, a hit is born. Take a look at some of today's chart-topping names: Billie Eilish, Dua Lipa, Lil Nas X. All these chart-topping artists are under the age of 30. While 30 doesn't *seem* old, in this business, it is. But you can be sure as soon as one act starts to grow up, there's another waiting to be born.

While today's musical acts age fast, the hits are here to stay. Pop music is true to its name—the biggest, best, and latest songs based on the results from the listening audience determine which songs get lumped into this genre. However, sometimes what's old is new. Rediscovery makes up for some of today's biggest musical hits. Fleetwood Mac's "Dreams" (1977) was discovered by an entire generation of TikTok-using teens when the '70s tune was featured in a viral video that racked up more than 30 million views on the social media app. That's not to say every piece of vinyl you have is going to be something your kids are going to love, but it just might be something you introduce them to one day. Bins of vinyl—paired with record players—are among the trendy and old-school items featured in some of the hottest stores for teens, such as Urban Outfitters. So, dust off the old turntable, drop the needle, and give your kids a history lesson that might solidify your hipster status in the process.

> **The Top 10 Genres in the Music Industry**
> Do you know what your kid likes?
> 1. *Pop*
> 2. *Hip Hop & Rap*
> 3. *Rock*
> 4. *Dance & Electronic Music*
> 5. *Latin Music*
> 6. *Indie & Alternative Rock*
> 7. *Classical Music*
> 8. *K-Pop*
> 9. *Country*
> 10. *Metal*
>
> Source: *Musician Wave*

SOCIAL MEDIA AS A MUSICAL GATEWAY

Not only does social media aid in creating the hits of today and reinventing classics, but it serves as a gateway for users to expand their horizons and become introduced to bands and genres that are making waves elsewhere. Just as Ed Sullivan introduced The Beatles to the world, laying the groundwork for

> **Best Video Game Music 2022**
> **Movies aren't the only things that have soundtracks now!**
> *God of War: Ragnarok*
> *Crisis Core: Final Fantasy VII Reunion*
> *Metal Hellsinger*
> *Xenoblade Chronicles 3*
> *CoD: Modern Warfare 2*
> Source: *Cog Connected*

the British Invasion to stir up a frenzy in the United States, social media has introduced Korean Pop, more commonly referred to as "K-Pop" to an entirely new audience. Groups such as BTS and BLACKPINK have found success in the U.S., from accruing multiple Billboard #1s to taking the stage at Coachella, respectively. The industry relies on acts like this to add diversity—both figuratively and literally—to the musical landscape of today. How many times can you stand to hear the same old song over and over again?

LISTEN

Social media and pop music are becoming more and more synonymous. Why? Think about who the majority of its users are—young people! That's who pop music is for, remember? Apps like TikTok, which relies heavily on the use of music and is the latest social media giant to gain staying power, have become the latest talent scouts responsible for making or breaking the songs of today (see "Dreams" above). The music industry relies on these social media metrics and popularity to pitch and popularize these records on the radio. Though they may not realize it, your kids are partially responsible for the decisions music executives are making—thanks to the song they used in the video of Dad setting the grill on fire. The good part about getting on apps like this? There's no age limit. Make an account and see for yourself what's out there. Using social media apps to gain a better understanding of today's musical landscape is the equivalent to tuning the dial to your local Top 40 station—only sometimes it may add more context or give a sneak preview as to why a certain song is played ten times a day. Scroll through the feed and keep yourself in the loop as to what's hot and what's not, as I can assure you that everyone from middle schoolers to record label SVPs are doing the same thing.

> ### Top Artists Year End 2022
> **Part of the fun is figuring out who will be tops during 2023!**
>
> *Bad Bunny*
> *Taylor Swift*
> *Harry Styles*
> *Drake*
> *Morgan Wallen*
> *Doja Cat*
> *Ed Sheeran*
> *Adele*
> *The Weeknd*
> *Lil Baby*
> *Future*
> *Justin Bieber*
> *Post Malone*
> *Jack Marlow*
> *Kendrick Lamar*
> *Luke Combs*
> *Juice WRLD*
> *Glass Animals*
> *Lil Durk*
> *Lil Nas X*
>
> Source: *Billboard*

TEEN PASSIONS & ACTIONS

LISTEN TO THE MUSIC

Music allows artists to express who they are and connect with listeners who may identify with their message. Whether it be about social issues or heart-wrenching breakups, find out who and what your kids are listening to, and see for yourself what they're singing about. As much as there is a business side to the music industry, filled with formulas and numbers that guarantee hits for the masses, there is a personal side to it that is unpredictable, and unique to each listener.

The best way to understand the music of today is to follow the steps of those it is directed toward. Get on social media. Listen to Top 40 radio. Ask what songs and artists are on your kids' playlists. Understand that you may not like it, but that's okay because it's not intended for you. And while the change in what teens are listening to may seem drastic, just remember that's not a bad thing. The music industry is a business, after all, and these changes and decisions are the consequences of their work. There are people choosing why certain songs are getting played. Whether it be because of social media, personal identification, or total shock-value, remember that there are professionals working behind the scenes, making calculated decisions as to what your kids are listening to.

NOAH CARUSO works in Pop/Rock Promotion at Atlantic Records.

WHY LIVE MUSIC MATTERS

By Summer Horvath

Concerts? This word is the meaning of my entire life. Since I was five years old, I have been attending and working concerts. Live music is my true meaning of happiness. My parents exposed me to music at such a young age. From air guitaring in the living room to singing my heart out at a live show, these opportunities were all because of my parents, who let me live my best life.

Please allow me to tell you a little story about the Jonas Brothers. This band gave me so much hope as a teen. I sang their songs in my bedroom and watched all their shows on the Disney Channel. When they announced a tour, my mom and sister said we couldn't afford it. My 12-year-old self was so sad until they surprised five of my friends and me with a limo to have what was then the best night of our lives. I remember walking in and being so amazed to see all these girls, just like me. So excited, anxious, and happy. My friends and I got glow sticks and t-shirts. And when the lights dimmed, I screamed all the way until the encore. Being a part of that crowd was something so momentous. I felt bigger than myself. I walked out with a badge of honor. I will never forget that night for as long as I live.

So, when people tell me that they have never been to a live show, I feel so unhappy for them because they have no idea what they are missing out on. Concerts have shaped me into the adult I am, they have given me an outlet to express myself, and they have taught me that you need to make memories in life. Because of the music and concerts my parents exposed me to as a kid, I decided I wanted my life's work to be in music. I started working in radio and attended a concert a week.

MAKING MEMORIES & BRINGING PEOPLE TOGETHER

Katrina Llapitan, regional promotions director at Audacy Las Vegas, Denver and Phoenix says, "I've been a part of live music for ten years now. If it's behind the scenes or in the crowd, it's always been a part of my life. Growing up with the music industry, I've seen the positive impact on what it can do for the younger generation. I hope that live music can continue to grow with society and be just as impactful then as it is now."

After working a concert a week and loving it, I got a job offer to work for Atlantic Records. Mo Hiromoto is the national senior director in Rhythm Promotion at Atlantic Records and describes live music this way: "Music is a universal language, so when you want to expose your kids to culture—music is the one thing that brings age, race, and ethnicity together. It brings everyone together from all walks of life. When you expose your kids to live music, you help them spread their wings. One of my favorite concert memories was going to the jazz fest as an adult with my

> 49% of teens report they have not been to a live concert. Of those, 38% say their parents have not let them. 42% of teens report that they want to go to a concert in 2023.
>
> Source: *Plugged-In Parent Survey of Teens*

dad in 2018. To this day, it is still my favorite memory. Doesn't matter what age, creed, or ethnicity—music brings people together."

And she is right. Music *is* a universal language. It helps bring a connection. Allow your child to make those memories. I know there can be risks, like the tragedy that occurred at Travis Scott's last show—but life is risk. Life is about going outside of your comfort zone and becoming the best version of yourself. And even if your heart is walking around on two legs, always remember you can accompany your kids. Allow yourself to create those memories *you* will never forget. And neither will your kids.

> Blast from the Past:
> **HIGHEST GROSSING CONCERTS**
> *1976 Elvis Presley*
> *1981 The Rolling Stones American Tour*
> *1985 Bruce Springsteen Born in the U.S.A. Tour*
> *1990 Madonna Blond Ambition Tour*
> *1995 Eagles Hell Freezes Over Tour*
> *2001 U2 Elevation Tour*

As Owen Smith, owner of the Miracle Theatre in Inglewood puts it, "Live music gives us the unique opportunity to share an artist's creation, and concerts allow us to connect with that living art. Attending concerts is fundamental to the greater human experience. Returning to live music with the general public in entertainment venues is reconnecting to ourselves." Safety is important, of course, and venues take that into serious consideration, but reconnecting with yourself is just as important.

I hope I have helped shape the perspective of live music and why it matters. Because it does. You know why? Because life is all about moments. And you can't miss out on this one.

SUMMER HORVATH works for Atlantic Records in Los Angeles, and is also a motivational speaker.

FAVORITE MUSICIANS, BANDS & GROUPS

The attention paid to the week's top songs or top artist may obscure parents' view of their own kids' favorites! In our survey, we asked teens to identify their favorite performing artist. As you can see, there is no consensus. So go ahead and ask your kids from time to time who their favorite performer is. They might surprise you.

BTS, King Von, Cardi B, João Gilberto, Lil Baby, Olivia Rodrigo, Juice wrld, BLACKPINK, Luke Bryan, Mitski, The Offspring, Taylor Swift, Lemon Demon, The Longest Johns, Will Wood, Billie Ellish, Morgan Walland, Eminem, Lana del Ray, Badflower, Ariana Grande, Olafur Arnalds, Rascal Flatts, Lil Nas X

Source: Plugged-In Parent Survey of Teens

COLLECT & TRADE

COLLECTING: WE'RE BEYOND THE CHECKLIST. WAY BEYOND.

By Nick Braccia

Ah, the plight of the young collector. As a '70s and '80s tyke, I just had to have every action figure listed on the back of the *Star Wars* packaging. And then it was G.I. Joe and He-Man, and then… you get the point. Naturally, this put my parents (and their checkbook) through hell, as every couple years I'd relegate dozens and dozens of toys to a basement or back-of-closet fate, where they still reside, like suburban temple relics, while I found some new endless inventory to amass.

And we're not even talking about all the baseball cards.

THE GACHAS SAY GOTCHA

Now, of course, I'm getting my comeuppance as the father of an eight-year-old girl. First with the Shopkins. That made sense. But then she abandoned them for more sophisticated fare and I was not ready for MGA Entertainment's L.O.L. Surprise dolls, which come in many varieties (girls, boys, teenagers, pets, fancy hair, etc) plus discrete and timed series releases, all with their own rarity schema (how hard it is to find certain dolls). In this brilliant business wrinkle—influenced by Japan's gacha games—the buyer, or the gift recipient, doesn't know what

COLLECT & TRADE

doll's in the package until they buy and open it. One may get a duplicate (and disappoint a child) or strike gold with an ultra-rare one (and disappoint an adult who would rather put it on eBay). It's a mechanism designed to get people to buy more, more, more in the hope of completing a collection. This is where the grey market comes into play.

THE GREY MARKET

Whether your child is collecting Magic: The Gathering cards, San Diego Comic-Con exclusives, or the aforementioned L.O.L.s, sometimes the only sure thing is the grey market—eBay, etc. You'll pay a pretty penny, but at least you'll take away the element of chance.

DIGITAL COLLECTING

Everything I've mentioned thus far is pretty standard and probably no surprise, but what about digital collecting, especially in metaverse worlds like Roblox, where my daughter now spends most of her waking hours? Or Fortnite, which is free to play, but commands big bucks for player avatars?

"Collecting" isn't as easy as checking off a list. There are constantly new items to wear, new pets to nurture, and new vehicles to race around. Some are unlocked via tedious grinding game play but many more can be purchased with in-game currency. This is where things can get a little crazy, as kids (and adults) click for that dopamine rush that comes with advancement and new items. Keep in mind, it's easy to manage allowances on these platforms—the feature is built into most of them—but know that, unlike with physical toys, there is NO GETTING TO THE END OF THE LIST. There will always be new digital items to procure, so make sure your kids understand the limit of their allowance and make purposeful choices. I don't have to tell you how many times I've had to look at my daughter's big, blue, sad eyes and tell her "No" when she demands another 400 Robux (about $5 worth).

The Walled Garden

The other issue with collecting digital items inside of applications that take a walled garden approach (this means you cannot use items you've paid for outside of their software), is that there is no simple way to sell the items if your child loses interest. It's a sunk cost. Fans and profiteers within Roblox and on other platforms do manage active digital grey markets, but it's a little tricky, for obvious reasons (wanting to maximize profits, fear of users scamming one another). But it's often the only way to guarantee getting a desired item.

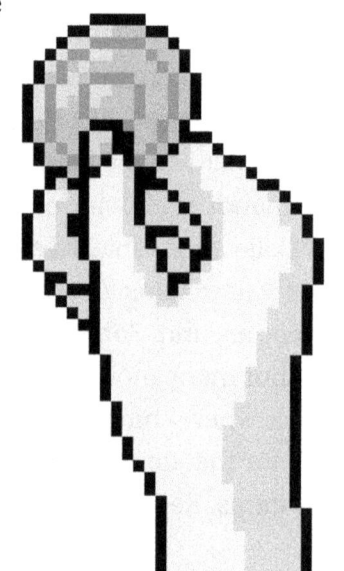

COLLECT & TRADE

HERE COME THE NFTS

Of course, everything I've just covered is about to (in the next three to five years) get bowled over by the fledgling world of NFTs (non-fungible tokens). One could write thousands of words about the recent history of these blockchain-based items. I'll try to be as clear as possible: if you convert dollars to a cryptocurrency (which is easy enough) and purchase an NFT, you own it. What does this mean for collectibles? For kids, the current market is not that interesting—high-priced art objects with little obvious function. But keep an eye on the space, because we're headed toward a world where, if you own an NFT of a character (we'll call him Ted the Knight) and you also own an NFT of a special sword for him, you may be able to carry that character, that sword, and all their characteristics from platform to platform. Game to game. It could be the end of walled gardens, where value builds and stays with your NFT character. Think of it as a coming shift in power from the platforms to the players (or collectors). In certain cases, you may also be able to write and publish stories about Ted the Knight and profit from them. If you're curious about this space, read up on Bored Ape Yacht Club and Forgotten Runes Wizards Cult, but keep in mind that the bottom for participation currently starts in the low four figures. And it gets higher quickly.

> **Brokerage Apps**
>
> It's never too young to start trading. But minors still need parental/guardian support to open an account. Help your kid get started on:
>
> *Robinhood*
> *Etrade*
> *Fidelity*

NICK BRACCIA is a Cannes Lions- and Clio-winning writer, director, and producer, and author of two books.

WHAT DO KIDS COLLECT & TRADE?

Though Pokémon and baseball cards remain popular, especially after the 2020 COVID-19 pandemic, the digital world provides many more trading options for tweens and teens. No, kids still can't open their own brokerage account, but with parental support they can. Here's the lowdown on what kids like to collect and trade.

VINYL

This may seem surprising with so many digital options, including Apple Music, Spotify, and Pandora Radio, just to name a few. But vinyl continues to be popular. There's even Vinyl TikTok. Who knows how this subset of TikTok users influenced sales? Regardless, being at home more has made it easier for kids to listen to records and share their collection with friends.

> **Top 5 Best-selling Vinyl Records of 2022**
> 1. Midnight *by Taylor Swift*
> 2. Harry's House *by Harry Styles*
> 3. Sour *by Olivia Rodrigo*
> 4. good kid, M.A.A.D. city *by Kendrick Lamar*
> 5. Rumors *by Fleetwood Mac*
>
> Source: *Statista*

SNEAKERS

Everyone loves a pair of comfortable and practical shoes. Some people love them a lot. Some people love them a lot a lot, enough to have numerous pairs or start a collection for a rare few. If you overhear the word "sneakerhead," look across the ground and, with some luck, you'll catch a glimpse of Nike Air Jordans, Air Force 1s, or Road Runners. According to Dictionary.com, a "sneakerhead" is "a person who collects and trades sneakers as a hobby, and who is typically knowledgeable about the history of sneakers." Netflix released a show about this type of kid, called *Sneakerheads*, which is on its second season. Even Sotheby's, the real-estate firm known for its luxury international listings, has a sneaker department now.

IN-GAME SKINS

These allow a player to change the appearance of their character, or their character's weapon, in a video game. Skins are solely aesthetic, having no gameplay function or utility. Players gain skins by finding them randomly, earning them through playing, or trading them. In Counter-Strike: Global Offensive (CSGO), not only can players "trade-up," swapping ten common skins for a more rare one, players can also trade amongst themselves. This is done using the trade function on Steam, the platform home to CSGO and other video games with skins. There's another option too—third party sites—where skins are traded for actual money. That's right, kids can take a slice of the multi-billion-dollar video gaming industry. If you've started to wonder about the legality of this, you're not alone. Recent years have seen several lawsuits, resulting mostly in stricter regulations. But there's usually a back door somewhere—Isle of Man, the almanac writers are looking at you. Skin betting sites (skin gambling) can be found elsewhere too, but the almanac editors do not condone or support this method. There are, however, legal alternatives.

CARDS

Baseball and Pokémon are classics. With more free time and nostalgia for old times during the pandemic, cards saw a surge in popularity.

NON-FUNGIBLE TOKENS (NFTS)

Digital tokens used to represent ownership of an item have taken the worlds of digital art and collectibles by storm. Tokens are secured by the Ethereum blockchain. Tokens can be designed but also minted from existing digital objects including GIFs, music, and videos. The minting process gives the token its utility. This means that in order to make an NFT, one needs to put forward the minting fee. After that, designers can sell their tokens and continue to reap royalties from sales. In the past few years, a lucky few Gen Zers have made millions off of their tokens.

Marketplaces

Here are a few standouts to buy and sell your items.

Amazon: Yes, you can resell your stuff on Amazon.

Facebook Marketplace: If you're looking for a real-world item or wanting to sell one, this is a good start.

Instagram Checkout: Launched in 2019, this helps both influencers and followers to sell and buy products without ever having to leave the platform on which they saw the stuff.

OpenSea: One of the largest markets for NFTs; also music NFTs and NFTs of collectibles, including cards and sports items.

SuperRare: Another option for buying and selling NFTs made by the world's top digital artists.

StockX: Mostly sneakers, but also trading cards, electronics, handbags, apparel, and other trendy items.

A TEENAGER'S GUIDE TO SNEAKER CULTURE

By Tryston Brown

Sneaker culture can quickly become a very important aspect of an adolescent's life. As they begin to grow up, an adolescent's idea of their appearance starts to change and becomes more focused. For most teens who are a part of sneaker culture, a nice pair of sneakers is often the centerpiece of their outfit, so it's a priority of ours to try to score a pair of these highly sought-after shoes. After the COVID-19 pandemic, popular shoes became even harder to find, because companies began selling shoes through online lotteries instead of having supplies of them in stores. Currently, the only way to get these shoes is through winning the lotteries, or paying expensive aftermarket values that could be double or even triple the original retail price of the shoe. Most people will take the option of waiting for a lottery win, especially if your child is trying to assemble a collection of these shoes.

HOW DOES A LOTTERY WORK?

There are many popular brands, but Jordan Brand's Air Jordans, Nike's Dunks, and Adidas's Yeezys tend to headline the most lotteries. Nike and Jordan lotteries and draws are done through the Nike SNKRS app, while Adidas uses the Confirmed app. Both SNKRS and Confirmed have calendars detailing which shoes will be releasing, their retail price, and the timeframe to enter the raffle. Raffles on SNKRS typically open up at 10:00 a.m. EST and close 10 minutes later. Adidas is a bit more unpredictable and can release at any time, so be sure to check the time listed by the shoe's profile. When the draw goes live, enter the size shoe you want and your shipping and payment information, then wait for the confirmation screen to show up. My pro tip is to fill out all of the necessary information ahead of time, because the extra five minutes it takes to input it could be the difference between winning or losing the draw.

The time it takes for the draw's results varies by the company. SNKRS will give you a screen with the words "GOT EM'" across it soon after the 10-minute period, if you secured the shoes. Confirmed will send a receipt sometime later on that day, if you won. If you lost, both companies will send pre-programmed messages bearing the bad news within 5 minutes. There is not much to do to increase your probability of winning other than interacting with the app's other media, and using

multiple accounts to enter. Chances are you won't win the first couple of draws, but if you use the app repeatedly, your first win should follow shortly after.

AN ALTERNATIVE MARKETPLACE

And what if you lose a lottery? You can always try the shoe marketplace, StockX. Most people use StockX to buy shoes, sell shoes, and to track the value of a given shoe. StockX is one of, if not the most popular, aftermarkets for shoes. It has gained this title because of its simple and straightforward interface, which gives you all of the information you need to know about a certain shoe. StockX also tends to set the tone for other third-party sellers' shoe costs as well. Enter the name of your desired shoe in the search bar, and StockX lists out prices for you to buy in every size, and prices that you could sell in every size. StockX also tells you the prices of what others are buying and selling for, the number of sales, the shoe's 12-month high and low prices, and graphs of these statistics. Because you are able to compare the statistics of different shoes, StockX makes it easy to identify trends so you can gain enough knowledge to make money reselling unworn shoes.

THE BENEFITS OF SNEAKER CULTURE

Overall, having a bit of sneaker knowledge makes it easy to start conversations and to connect with your child, and for your child to connect with other people. I have found that showing up to school with a new pair of shoes gives me a glow of confidence, whenever I step into a classroom. The excitement and compliments about a pair of shoes from one sneaker lover to another will typically be reciprocated by another member of the community. When this cycle repeats, it creates positive bonds and maybe even some new friendships. It's amazing to see what sneakers can bring out in people. The big takeaway here is that the sneaker community can be enjoyable, whether you only know the basics or are deeply immersed in it.

TRYSTON BROWN is a high school sophomore who lives and breathes sneakers.

Blast from the Past: **TOP COLLECTIBLES**

1975
Toy Cars
Baseball Cards
Comic Books

1980s
Cabbage Patch Kids
Transformers
Game Boy
Ninja Turtle Action Figures
Thundercats
Furby

1990s
Tamagochi
POG
Barbie
Yu-Gi-Oh Cards
Pokémon Cards
Tech Decks
Polly Pocket
Bop It
Sky Dancers
Yo-Yos

2000s
Toy Cars
Hello Kitty
Snoopy
Simpsons Toys
Zizzle Happy Meal Toy
Superhero Action Figures
Funko Pop

SHOW OFF A STYLE
Beauty & Fashion

A PARENT'S GUIDE TO FASHION & BEAUTY TRENDS

As the temperature shifts, many people know trends come and go. Fashion continues to reinvent itself, borrowing vintage styles and revamping them. Not only do fashion trends grace magazine spreads, now more than ever they are found on social media. Social media has also become a hotspot for beauty trends, tips, and tricks. Below are fashion and beauty trends from this past year that may well extend into 2022, as well as predictions about the upcoming year.

SUMMER 2023 FASHION TRENDS

Fresh off of the spring runway collections, 2023's biggest fashion trends are here. According to Refinery29, here are seven trends to shop for summer.

Red: From head to toe, look for juicy reds with an orange undertone.

Cargo Pants: Utilitarian wear with tailored cuts, interesting colors, and elevated fabrics.

Sheer Clothing: From the red carpet and street wear to workwear and your weekend clothes, sheer is no longer risqué.

Denim Reimagined: In addition to double-waisted and carpenter jeans, think also strapless dresses, shirting, and shoes.

Maxi Skirts: They're here to stay.

Blast from the Past: **TOP FASHION BRANDS**

1975
Geoffrey Beene
Calvin Klein

1980
Jordache
Wrangler
Levi's
Sasson
Ray-Ban
Puma
Converse
Benetton

1985
Jams
Sperry
Swatch
Ray-Ban

1990s
FUBU
Ecko Unltd.
Sean John
Pepe Jeans
Joe Boxer
Billabong
Diesel
Gap
Reebok
Nike
DKNY
Polo

2000
Juicy Couture
Abercrombie & Fitch

TEEN PASSIONS & ACTIONS

2023 BEAUTY TRENDS

According to *Her Campus*, here are some trends to look forward to in 2023.

The Pink Glam Look: Bright blushes, lip stains, and cheek highlights.

Bold Makeup: Rebellious dark, bold makeup in everyday looks.

Apricot Makeup: A warm pop of color to your eyes, cheeks, or lips.

Glazed Makeup: This glowy look can be fresh and natural for daytime or glamorous and radiant for night.

Natural Lashes: Move towards a good mascara rather than big false lashes.

Hair Swirl: A unique way to style your bangs reminiscent of the 60s-mod era.

French Ombré Nails: A modern twist on the French manicure that can be glazed, glittery, or pastel.

SHOW OFF A STYLE

Blast from the Past: **MAKEUP TRENDS**

1975

Glitter Eyeshadow
Red Lips
Contouring
1920s Revival: brows, lips, eyes
Smoky Eye
Art Deco Looks
Punk Trends: dark eyeshadow, pale skin

1980s

Bold and Dramatic
Heavy Eyeshadow, covering the entire eye space
Contrasting Colors
Pink Blushes
Blues and Purples

1990s

Natural Look or Heavy Eyeliner
Clear or Tinted Lip Gloss
Brown Eyeshadows, drawing attention to the eyes

2000

Nude Lips
Bold Brows
No-makeup Makeup
Subtle Winged Eyeliner

TEEN PASSIONS & ACTIONS

FALL 2023 FASHION TRENDS

As the weather turns chillier, here are Fall 2023 trends to look out for from *Marie Claire*.

1. Classic Tailoring
2. Red (Again!)
3. Dark Romance
4. Leather Sets
5. Short Shorts
6. Sheer Paneling
7. Decorative Bras
8. Circle Skirts
9. Butter Yellow
10. Shearling Outerwear
11. Wardrobe Basics (classic button-up shirts, oversized blazers, wide-leg jeans)
12. Fruit-themed Clothing and Accessories

WINTER 2023–2024 FASHION TRENDS

Fashion Network has compiled a list based on the 2023–2024 ready-to-wear collections that highlight a strong woman borrowing from a man's wardrobe.

Skirt Suits: Cut from traditional men's fabrics or unexpected materials like knitwear, skirt suits are returning to a refined silhouette.

New Formal Skirt: A flared corolla skirt with a wasp waist.

Bustier: Worn over a shirt or jacket to enhance the waist or on its own, bustiers fit all shapes and sizes.

Dots and Studs: White polka dots on black backgrounds return from the 1950s, or replacing the dots with some metallic finishes like studs and eyelets.

Tights and Shorts: The no skirt and pant trend will prevail through the winter with opaque tights and short shorts.

Men's Briefs: Pull them on under a chic sheer skirt.

Cropped Cuts: From outerwear to sweatshirts and sweaters.

Ties: Worn simple with a white shirt, tone on tone, or undone like a scarf.

TEEN PASSIONS & ACTIONS

TIKTOK BEAUTY TRENDS

No sartorially conscious person can overestimate the value of beauty products, tricks, and trends. For this reason, we've found some lists of TikTok trends and products.

According to *Teen Vogue*, these are some must-have products (and their associated trends):

e.l.f. Glossy Lip Stains: This low-effort product can be applied and blotted once and last throughout the day.

Rare Beauty Soft Pinch Liquid Blush: Created by Selena Gomez, a little goes a long way and blends perfectly.

Etude House SoonJung 2x Barrier Intensive Cream: Hypoallergenic and fragrance-free it's ideal for hydrating sensitive skin.

Essence Glimmer Glow Lipstick: Affordable and cruelty-free, this goes on clear but leaves a glitter and sparkle tint.

NFX Professional Makeup Bare With Me Hydrating Face & Body Concealer Serum: Available in 13 shades and $11.

REFY Brow Sculpt Shape and Hold Gel with Lamination Effect: Get your laminated brows without the chemical process.

SHOW OFF A STYLE

Blast from the Past: **TOP HAIRSTYLES**

1975

The Farrah Fawcett
Short-feathered Cuts
Shag Bangs/Cuts
The Wedge
Afros
Asymmetrical Cuts
Shaved Heads
Mohicans (hair horns)
Perms

1980s

The Mullet
Tall Mohawks
Jheri Curls
Flattops
High Top Fades
Perms
Spiked Hair

1990s

The Rachel
Crimped Waves
Butterfly Clips
Zigzag Headbands
High Ponytails
Pigtails
Tight Curls
Messy Buns

2000s

Wavy Hair
Bangs Pinned to the Side
Curled/Crimped Combo
Layered Hair
Piecey Bangs
Bandanas
Flipped-out Ends
Hair Poufs
Spiky Hair
Zigzag Parts
Side Bangs
Face-framing Tendrils
Chunky Highlights

Top Fashion & Beauty Retailers for Teens

Gen Z shops fast fashion. And we mean fast. Retailers like ASOS drop at least 5,000 new styles a week and SHEIN offers 700 to 1,000 new styles daily. SHEIN is now the largest fast fashion retailer in the U.S., comprising 28% of sales, surpassing H&M (20%), and Zara (11%). SHEIN's success is attributed to its low prices (e.g., $5 crop tops, $15 dresses), newness, and an army of social media influencers. And SHEIN has taken the crown from Amazon as the No. 1 app in the shopping categories on IOS and Android.

Other such retailers attracting teens are: Zara, Top Shop, H&M, and PrettyLittleThing. (By the way, fast fashion brands are not considered environmentally sustainable, if that matters in your household.)

Yet teens are also embracing thrift stores. Secondhand and consignment e-commerce marketplaces, such as thredUP, Swap.com, depop, Poshmark, Tradesy, and The RealReal, can be a source of purchases, income, and fun.

All of the below lists are based on a 2021 survey by Piper Sandler; percentages refer to percent of surveyed teens who listed the retailer as their No. 1.

> **Spending Preferences**
>
> If they had $100 to spend, teens' preference is to spend it on jewelry, then clothes, and then shoes.
>
> Source: *Plugged-In Parent Survey of Teens*

What are the top online retailers for teens in the U.S.?

1. Amazon, 52%
2. SHEIN, 9%
3. Nike, 5%
4. PacSun, 4%

SHOW OFF A STYLE

What are the top clothing retailers for teens in the U.S.?

1. Nike, 27%
2. American Eagle, 7%
3. PacSun, 5%
4. Adidas, 5%
5. Lululemon, 5%

What are the top beauty retailers for teens in the U.S.?

1. Ulta, 46%
2. Sephora, 21%
3. Target, 10%
4. Walmart, 7%
5. Amazon, 3%

What are the top footwear retailers for teens in the U.S.?

1. Nike, 57%
2. Vans, 11%
3. Adidas, 9%
4. Converse, 7%
5. Foot Locker, 2%

GET TO KNOW BEAUTY INFLUENCERS

By Becky Pham

beauty influencers, also known as *beauty gurus* or *beauty vloggers*, are typically young individuals who create content on YouTube and other social media (such as Instagram, TikTok, and Snapchat) to offer advice on makeup, skin care, fashion, and lifestyle.

Alongside the rise of social media use among youth, beauty influencers are reshaping the beauty industry with their online presence.

Replacing print teen magazines that have largely disappeared, beauty influencers have become the new gatekeepers and brand ambassadors who select which cosmetics products are featured and reviewed for their audience at a faster speed, with highly appealing visuals and sounds. Through short-lived content that goes viral, social media and beauty influencers can cause certain cosmetics products to be sold out for weeks, as youth follow these trends to recreate the look for themselves.

WHAT IS ONLINE BEAUTY CONTENT?

Beauty-related content on YouTube is big business. It has grown from just 130 million views in 2006 to 169 billion views in 2018.

Notable Types of Beauty-related Videos on YouTube

Makeup tutorial	Teaching viewers how to apply makeup, from full face to specific makeup areas (such as eyebrows, eyeliners, eyelashes, blushes, lips, etc.)
Celebrity makeup tutorial	Teaching viewers how to apply makeup in order to resemble a celebrity (such as Angelina Jolie, Taylor Swift, etc.)
Makeup challenge	Showing viewers how to fulfill a makeup look with certain constraints (such as limited time, only using kids makeup, only using one cosmetics brand, etc.)
Makeup product review	Offering personal commentary on the quality, price, and design of cosmetics products and brands
Makeup shopping vlog	Showing viewers footage of how the beauty influencer goes out and shops for cosmetics
Makeup swatch	Showing viewers how the beauty influencer applies multiple samples of cosmetics products (such as lipstick, face foundation, etc.) on their skin to test the products' colors
Makeup product haul	Showing viewers a large number of cosmetics products that the beauty influencer has purchased during a particular time
Q&A	The beauty influencer answers questions submitted online by their viewers (the content might or might not be related to beauty products)
Story time	The beauty influencer tells interesting, if not random, stories about their life and content (the content might or might not be related to beauty products)

HOW HAVE BEAUTY INFLUENCERS CHANGED OVER THE YEARS?

The beauty influencer community on YouTube started around 2006, with the first content creators focusing on makeup techniques and tips, especially those inspired by television characters and celebrities.

In the early 2010s, newer content creators started to feature individual cosmetics products, brands, and trends more heavily. These popular video types (such as review videos, product hauls, and makeup challenges) have since then catapulted beauty influencers to the forefront of YouTube content.

Compared to these earlier times, beauty influencers of the early 2020s are very different. The age of the old-school, girl-next-door "get ready with me" makeup tutorial is long gone. Beauty influencers of today can be roughly categorized into three major groups, the *superstar*, the *popular*, and the *smaller* influencers.

The Superstar Influencers

A very small group of beauty influencers have become very successful on YouTube, with billions of views. They have established their own cosmetics brands and resemble Hollywood celebrities in their popularity.

The **superstar** influencers often possess and embody big money, lavish lifestyles, high-end products, dramatic personalities, and high-profile scandals with massive numbers of (anti-)fans.

For example, between 2020 and 2021, Jeffree Star was ranked in Forbes' list of Highest-Paid YouTube Stars, while Shane Dawson and James Charles were reportedly accused of pedophilia and underage sexting with their fans.

Some superstars have recently been embroiled in feuds amongst themselves that attracted news headlines. With much less focus on beauty tips or products, they have exposed one another's secrets or accused one another of misconduct on social media.

The Popular Influencers

The **popular** beauty influencers secure their popularity with stable view counts and a solid fanbase.

With less celebrity power and less controversy than the superstars, the popular influencers often focus significantly on beauty-related content and knowledge, with just as much fun and appealing visuals.

They also typically have their own brands of cosmetics and lifestyle products, although more recently launched than those by the superstars.

The Smaller Influencers

With less media attention and view counts than the superstars and the popular influencers, the **smaller** influencers are often newer or up-and-coming players in the beauty influencer community.

Instead of focusing on the lavish and high-profile lifestyle appeal, they more often feature affordable and relatable cosmetics brands, such as those from drugstores.

The smaller influencers might have partnerships with major cosmetics brands, but have not necessarily launched a brand under their own names.

Notable Beauty Influencers

SUPERSTAR INFLUENCERS

NAME/YOUTUBE CHANNEL NAME	SUBSCRIBERS	VIEW COUNTS
James Charles (jamescharles)	24.4 million	3.5 billion
Jeffree Star (jeffreestar)	16.2 million	2.5 billion
Nikkie de Jager (NikkieTutorials)	13.9 million	1.5 billion
Bretman Rock (BretmanRock)	8.8 million	559 million
Tati Westbrook (Tati)	8.69 million	1.4 billion

NOTABLE POPULAR INFLUENCERS

NAME/YOUTUBE CHANNEL NAME	SUBSCRIBERS	VIEW COUNTS
Hyram (Hyram)	4.59 million	376 million
Jackie Aina (JackieAina)	3.57 million	385 million
Kristi (RawBeautyKristi)	1.22 million	155 million
Emily Noel (emilynoel83)	1 million	223 million
Sarah Cheung (Sacheu)	802k	55 million

NOTABLE SMALLER INFLUENCERS

NAME/YOUTUBE CHANNEL NAME	SUBSCRIBERS	VIEW COUNTS
Andréa Matillano (AndreaMatillano)	331k	53 million
JUDY (JudyReviews)	140k	17 million
Tina (thefancyface)	104k	12 million
Lauren Mae (LaurenMaeBeauty)	100k	17 million
Kelly Gooch (KellyGooch)	82.6k	14 million

SHOW OFF A STYLE

PARENTING CHECKLIST

When it comes to online content created by beauty influencers:

- Talk to your child to understand why they find it appealing.

- Note which group of influencers (the superstar, the popular, or the smaller influencers) your child tends to watch and follow.

- Diversify your child's content consumption from the other group(s) of influencers.

- Encourage your child to cultivate a passion for the arts.

- Encourage your child to hone their makeup craft through self-study.

- Encourage your child's self-motivation through beauty influencers' success stories.

- Encourage your child to spot brand endorsements.

- Beware of your child's increased consumerism through brand endorsements.

- Beware of your child's potential body sexualization through online beauty trends.

- Beware of your child's potential eating disorders through online beauty trends.

BECKY PHAM, MA, is a PhD student in communication at the University of Southern California.

THE COST OF RAISING A TEENAGER

Monthly Cost of Raising a Teen in the U.S.

CATEGORY	COST (RANGE)	COST (AVERAGE)
Housing	$200 (rural) – $325 (urban)	$262.50
Food	$171.35 – $366.20	$275.48
Transportation	$132.92 – $248.33	$190.63
Health Care	$73.75 – 148.33	$111.04
Clothing	$60.83 – $107.92	$84.38
Child Care/Education (not incl. college)	$45 – $440.83	$242.92
Misc.	$47.50 – $147.50	$97.50
TOTAL:	$731.35 – $1,784.11	$1,264.45

SHOW OFF A STYLE

Beauty Routine

DRUGSTORE BRANDS

CATEGORY	SUBCATEGORY	BRAND	PRICE	SIZE
Skin Care	Face Wash	Neutrogena Fresh Foaming Cleanser	$5.29	6.7 fl oz
	Toner	Garnier SkinActive Micellar Cleansing Water	$3.49	3.4 oz
	Exfoliant	St. Ives Energizing Scrub - Coconut & Coffee	$3.99	6 oz
	Moisturizer	Cetaphil Oil-Free Hydrating Lotion	$12.19	3 fl oz
	Sunscreen	Neutrogena Clear Face Liquid Sunscreen Lotion	$10.99	3 fl oz
	Acne Spot Cream	Neutrogena On-the-Spot Acne Treatment	$6.47	0.75 oz
	Makeup Remover	Neutrogena Makeup Remover Cleansing Towelettes & Face Wipes	$4.99	
		Budget Skin Care Total	**$47.41**	
Hair Care	Shampoo	L'Oreal Paris Elvive Total Repair 5 Repairing Shampoo for Damaged Hair	$3.42	12.6 fl oz
	Conditioner	L'Oreal Paris Elvive Total Repair 5 Repairing Conditioner for Damaged Hair	$3.42	12.6 fl oz
	Hair Brush	Wet Brush Original Hair Brush	$7.27	
	Heat Protectant	Tresemme Thermal Creations Heat Tamer Spray	$6.99	8 oz
	Hairspray	Rave Unscented Hairspray	$1.97	11 oz
	Hair Dryer	Revlon Essentials Compact and Lightweight Cold Shot Button Hair Dryer	$9.34	
	Flat Iron	Remington Anti-Static Flat Iron	$19.84	
	Curling Iron	Conair Instant Heat Curling Iron, 1.25	$13.97	
		Budget Hair Care Total	**$66.22**	

TEEN PASSIONS & ACTIONS

CATEGORY	SUBCATEGORY	BRAND	PRICE	SIZE
Makeup	Makeup Brushes	EcoTools Makeup Brush Set	$9.98	
	Primer	Rimmel Stay Matte Primer	$3.63	1 fl oz
	Foundation	Maybelline Fit Me! Matte & Poreless Foundation	$3.15	1 fl oz
	Concealer	Maybelline Instant Age Rewind Eraser Multi-Use Concealer	$4.33	0.2 fl oz
	Blush	Rimmel Maxi Blush	$4.28	0.31 oz
	Eyebrows	Maybelline TattooStudio Tattoo Brow 36HR Pigment Brow Pencil	$6.98	0.026 oz
	Eyeshadow	e.l.f. Cosmetics Bite Size Eyeshadow Palette	$3.00	0.12 oz
	Eyeliner	NYX Professional Makeup Retractable Mechanical Eyeliner Pencil	$5.50	0.01 oz
	Mascara	COVERGIRL Professional All In One Curved Brush Mascara	$5.44	0.3 fl oz
	Lip Gloss	NYX Professional Makeup Butter Gloss	$4.97	0.27 oz
		Budget Makeup Total	**$51.26**	
Nails	Manicure Kit	Ulta Manicure Kit	$12.00	
	Nail Polish	L.A. Colors Color Last Nail Polish	$1.98	0.5 fl oz
	Top Coat	"L.A. Colors Color Last Nail Polish, Crystal Top Coat"	$1.98	0.5 fl oz
	Nail Polish Remover	Cutex Ultra-Powerful Nail Polish Remover	$1.99	6.7 oz
		Budget Nails Total	**$17.95**	
		BUDGET BEAUTY ROUTINE TOTAL	$182.84	

SHOW OFF A STYLE

POPULAR BRANDS

CATEGORY	SUBCATEGORY	BRAND	PRICE	SIZE
Skin Care	Face Wash	Glossier Cleanser Concentrate	$20	3.3 fl oz
	Toner	Thayers Alcohol-Free Witch Hazel Facial Toner	$10.95	12 oz
	Exfoliant	Aveeno Positively Radiant Skin Brightening Daily Scrub	$5.89	5 oz
	Moisturizer	CeraVe Daily Moisturizing Body and Face Lotion	$12.99	8 oz
	Sunscreen	Glossier Invisible Shield	$25	1 fl oz
	Acne Spot Cream	Mario Badescu Drying Lotion	$17	1 oz
	Makeup Remover	Burt's Bees Micellar Makeup Removing Towelettes With Rose Water	$5.99	
		Popular Skin Care Total	**$97.82**	
Hair Care	Shampoo	OGX Thick & Full + Biotin & Collagen Shampoo	$7.99	13 oz
	Conditioner	OGX Thick & Full Biotin & Collagen Conditioner	$7.99	13 oz
	Hair Brush	Drybar Detangling Brush	$20	
	Heat Protectant	Redken Extreme Play Safe Heat Protection and Damage Repair Treatment	$25	6.8 oz
	Hair Spray	Redken Fashion Work 12 Medium Hold Hairspray	$21	9.8 oz
	Hair Dryer	InfinitiPro by Conair Salon Professional Hair Dryer	$24.99	
	Flat Iron	Conair Infiniti Pro Rainbow Titanium Flat Iron	$44.99	
	Curling Iron	Hot Tools Professional Gold Curling Iron	$49.99	
		Popular Hair Care Total	**$201.95**	

TEEN PASSIONS & ACTIONS

CATEGORY	SUBCATEGORY	BRAND	PRICE	SIZE
Makeup	Makeup Brushes	BH Cosmetics Signature Rose Gold - 13 Piece Brush Set	$26	
	Primer	Benefit Cosmetics The POREfessional Pore Minimizing Primer	$32	0.75 oz
	Foundation	MAC Studio Fix Fluid SPF 15 Foundation	$35	1 oz
	Concealer	Tarte Shape Tape Concealer	$29	0.33 oz
	Blush	Cover FX Monochromatic Blush Duo	$38	0.51 oz
	Eyebrows	Benefit Cosmetics Precisely, My Brow Pencil Waterproof Eyebrow Definer	$24	0.002 oz
	Eyeshadow	Anastasia Beverly Hills Norvina Eyeshadow Palette	$45	0.28 oz
	Eyeliner	Urban Decay Cosmetics 24/7 Glide-On Waterproof Eyeliner Pencil	$22	0.04 oz
	Mascara	Too Faced Better Than Sex Volumizing Mascara	$27	0.27 oz
	Lip Gloss	Buxom Full-On Plumping Lip Polish	$21	0.15 oz
		Popular Makeup Total	**$299.00**	
Nails	Manicure Kit	Flowery Nailit Pro Manicure Kit	$15	
	Nail Polish	OPI Nature Strong Natural Origin Nail Lacquer	$11.50	0.5 oz
	Top Coat	Seche Dry Fast Top Coat	$9.95	0.5 oz
	Nail Polish Remover	Zoya Remove+ Nail Polish Remover	$10	8 oz
		Popular Nails Total	**$46.45**	
		POPULAR BEAUTY ROUTINE TOTAL	**$645.22**	

SHOW OFF A STYLE

LUXURY BRANDS

CATEGORY	SUBCATEGORY	BRAND	PRICE	SIZE
Skin Care	Face Wash	La Mer The Cleansing Foam	$95	4.2 oz
	Toner	SK-II Facial Treatment Essence	$185	5.4 oz
	Exfoliant	La Mer The Replenishing Oil Exfoliator	$135	3.4 oz
	Moisturizer	La Mer Crème de la Mer Moisturizer	$190	1 oz
	Sunscreen	Hourglass Equilibrium™ Day Fluid Sunscreen Broad Spectrum SPF 30	$105	1.7 oz
	Acne Spot Cream	Kate Somerville EradiKate® Salicylic Acid Acne Treatment	$60	1 oz
	Makeup Remover	Koh Gen Do Cleansing Spa Water Makeup Remover	$66	12.85 oz
		Luxury Skin Care Total	**$836.00**	
Hair Care	Shampoo	Oribe Shampoo for Brilliance & Shine	$49	8.5 oz
	Conditioner	Oribe Conditioner for Brilliance & Shine	$52	6.8 oz
	Hair Brush	Christophe Robin Boar Bristle Detangling Paddle Hairbrush	$108	
	Heat Protectant	Oribe Royal Blowout Heat Styling Spray	$69	5.9 oz
	Hairspray	Oribe Superfine Hair Spray	$42	9 oz
	Hair Dryer	ghd Air 1600W Professional Hair Dryer	$199	
	Flat Iron	ghd Classic Styler - 1" Flat Iron	$149	
	Curling Iron	ghd Classic Curl - 1" Curling Iron	$199	
		Luxury Hair Care Total	**$867.00**	

TEEN PASSIONS & ACTIONS

CATEGORY	SUBCATEGORY	BRAND	PRICE	SIZE
Makeup	Makeup Brushes	Sephora Collection PRO 6-Piece Brush Set	$85	
	Primer	Yves Saint Laurent Touche Eclat Blur Face Primer	$52	1 oz
	Foundation	La Mer The Soft Fluid Long Wear Foundation SPF 20	$135	1 oz
	Concealer	Tom Ford Emotionproof Concealer	$54	0.24 fl oz
	Blush	Tom Ford Shade & Illuminate Blush Duo	$90	0.22 oz
	Eyebrows	Tom Ford Brow Sculptor	$54	0.02 oz
	Eyeshadow	Natasha Denona Eyeshadow Palette 28	$239	
	Eyeliner	Tom Ford Eye Defining Pen Liquid Eyeliner Duo	$59	0.03 oz
	Mascara	Lancôme Lash Idôle Lash-Lifting & Volumizing Mascara	$26	0.27 fl oz
	Lip Gloss	Tom Ford Gloss Luxe Lip Gloss	$57	0.24 oz
		Luxury Makeup Total	**$851.00**	
Nails	Manicure Kit	Sephora Collection Manicure Nail Tool Kit	$24	
	Nail Polish	Deborah Lippmann Gel Lab Pro Nail Polish	$20	0.5 oz
	Top Coat	Deborah Lippmann Gel Lab Pro - Nail Base Coat and Top Coat Set	$45	0.5 oz x2
	Nail Polish Remover	NAILS INC. Gel-less Gel Nail Polish Remover Kit	$19	
		Luxury Nails Total	**$108.00**	
		LUXURY BEAUTY ROUTINE TOTAL	**$2,662.00**	

Sources: The above prices were identified from multiple sources and may no longer be current. Please check retailers for current prices.

SHOW OFF A STYLE

Back to School Outfit

THRIFTED - GIRLS ONLINE

CATEGORY	BRAND	PRICE
Top	Brandy Melville	$9.99 + $5.99 shipping
Jeans	Hollister	$10.99 + $5.99 shipping
Jacket	Lazer Jeans	$15.99 + $5.99 shipping
Socks (pack of 3)	Old Navy	$15 + $3.99 shipping
Sandals	Qupid	$10.99 + $5.99 shipping
Sneakers	Adidas	$32.99 + $5.99 shipping
Necklace	N/A	$15 + $3.99 shipping
Bracelet	N/A	$5 + $3.99 shipping
Earrings	N/A	$11 + $3.99 shipping
	Girls Thrifted Online Total	$111.95 + shipping

THRIFTED - GIRLS IN-STORE

CATEGORY	BRAND	PRICE
Top	N/A	$4.49
Jeans	N/A	$5.99
Jacket	N/A	$6.99
Socks (1 pair)	N/A	$0.49
Shoes	N/A	$5.99
Jewelry	N/A	$9.99
	Girls Thrifted In-Store Total	$33.94

THRIFTED - BOYS ONLINE

CATEGORY	BRAND	PRICE
Shirt	Hollister	$15 + $3.99 shipping
Jeans	American Eagle	$18 + $3.99 shipping
Jacket	Adidas	$26 + $3.99 shipping
Socks (pack of 4)	Under Armour	$18 + $3.99 shipping
Sneakers	Converse	$30 + $3.99 shipping
Athletic Shoes	Adidas	$35 + $3.99 shipping
Belt	Columbia	$15 + $3.99 shipping
	Boys Thrifted Online Total	$157 + shipping

TEEN PASSIONS & ACTIONS

THRIFTED - BOYS IN-STORE

CATEGORY	BRAND	PRICE
Shirt	N/A	$4.49
Jeans	N/A	$5.99
Jacket	N/A	$6.99
Socks (1 pair)	N/A	$0.49
Shoes	N/A	$5.99
Belt	N/A	$1.99
	Boys Thrifted In-Store Total	$25.94

NEW FROM MALL - GIRLS

CATEGORY	BRAND	PRICE
Top	Aeropostale	$29.95
Jeans	American Eagle	$59.95
Jacket	Old Navy	$59.99
Socks (pack of 3)	Old Navy	$9.99
Sandals	Forever 21	$15.99
Sneakers	Adidas	$85.00
Necklace	H&M	$5.99
Bracelet	Forever 21	$6.99
Earrings	H&M	$5.99
	Girls Mall Total	$279.84

NEW FROM MALL - BOYS

CATEGORY	BRAND	PRICE
Shirt	Hollister	$29.95
Jeans	American Eagle	$59.95
Jacket	Old Navy	$69.99
Socks (pack of 3)	Nike	$18
Sneakers	Vans	$49.95
Athletic Shoes	Adidas	$75
Belt	American Eagle	$24.95
	Boys Mall Total	$327.79

SHOW OFF A STYLE

HIGH END - GIRLS

CATEGORY	BRAND	PRICE
Top	Free People	$108
Jeans	Rag & Bone	$225
Jacket	Calvin Klein	$229
Socks (pack of 2)	UGG	$32
Sandals	Tory Burch	$228
Sneakers	Michael Kors	$165
Necklace	Tiffany	$350
Bracelet	Gucci	$200
Earrings	Valentino	$290
	High End Girls Total	$1,827.00

HIGH END - BOYS

CATEGORY	BRAND	PRICE
Shirt	Polo Ralph Lauren	$98.50
Jeans	Diesel	$195
Jacket	Calvin Klein	$262
Socks	Calvin Klein	$14
Sneakers	Adidas Yeezy	$319
Athletic Shoes	Nike	$275
Belt	Gucci	$480
	High End Boys Total	$1,643.50

Sources: The above prices were identified from multiple sources and may no longer be current. Please check retailers for current prices.

New Game Setup

PLAYSTATION 5

ITEM	PRICE
Console	$499.99
Console Digital Edition (no disk drive)	$359.99
Extra Wireless Controller	$69.99
Pulse 3D Wireless Headset	$99.99
DualSense Controller Charging Station	$29.99
HD Camera	$59.99
PlayStation Plus - 12 mo subscription	$59.99
PS5 game	$19.99-$89.99

PLAYSTATION 4

ITEM	PRICE
Console	$299.99
Pro Console	$348.68
Extra Wireless Controller	$59.99
Turtle Beach Headset	$59.99
Camera	$59.99
PlayStation Plus - 12 mo subscription	$59.99
PS4 game	$9.99-$259.99

XBOX SERIES X/S

ITEM	PRICE
Console (X)	$499.99
Console (S)	$299.99
SD Card Upgrade	$219.99
Extra Controller	$59.99
Rechargable Battery	$24.44
Headset	$59.99
Xbox Live Gold - 1 year (charged quarterly)	$99.96
Xbox Game Pass Ultimate (includes Xbox Gold) - 1 year (charged monthly)	$165.89
Xbox X/S Game	$9.99-$119.99

XBOX ONE S

ITEM	PRICE
Console	$499.99
SD Card Upgrade	$219.99
Extra Controller	$59.99
Rechargable Battery	$24.44
Headset	$59.99
Xbox Live Gold - 1 year (charged quarterly)	$99.96
Xbox Game Pass Ultimate (includes Xbox Gold) - 1 year (charged monthly)	$165.89
Xbox One S Game	$9.99-$119.99

SHOW OFF A STYLE

NINTENDO SWITCH

ITEM	PRICE
Console - OLED	$349.99
Console - Original	$299.99
Console - Lite (handheld only)	$199.99
Extra Joy-Con Set	$79.99
Pro Controller	$69.99
Nintendo Switch Online - 12 mo subscription (charged yearly)	$19.99
Nintendo Switch Game	$0-$119.99

OCULUS QUEST 2

ITEM	PRICE
VR Headset (128 GB)	$299
VR Headset (256 GB)	$399
Carrying Case	$49
Elite Strap	$49
Link Cable	$79
Charging Dock	$99
Oculus Quest Game	$0-$39.99

Sources: The above prices were identified from multiple sources and may no longer be current. Please check retailers for current prices.

First Concert Experience

TAYLOR SWIFT

ITEM	PRICE
Ticket - Low Price	$175
Ticket - Average Price	$221
Ticket - High Price (near stage)	$1,500
Floor VIP Package	$4,000
Pit VIP Package	$4,500
Album Vinyl	$26
Sweatshirt	$60
T-Shirt	$30
Cup Set	$20
Metallic Tattoo Set	$12
Ring	$35

JUSTIN BIEBER

ITEM	PRICE
Ticket - Low Price	$145
Ticket - Average Price	$230
Ticket - High Price (near stage)	$574
Diamond VIP Experience Ticket (backstage tour, photo with Justin Bieber, complementary merchandise, etc.)	$1,549
Short Sleeve T-Shirt	$35
Long-Sleeve Crewneck Shirt	$65
Hoodie	$70
Trucker Hat	$30
Sticker Pack	$20

TEEN PASSIONS & ACTIONS

ARIANA GRANDE

ITEM	PRICE
Ticket - Low Price	$33
Ticket - Average Price	$255
Ticket - High Price	$525
Premium VIP Front Row Ticket	$850
Crewneck T-Shirt	$35
Crewneck Sweatshirt	$70
Coffee Mug	$15
Poster	$15

BILLIE EILISH

ITEM	PRICE
Ticket - Low Price	$95
Ticket - Average Price	$645.83
Ticket - VIP	$1,520
Ticket - Most Expensive	$8,505
Billie Eilish x Air Jordan Shoes	$170
Hoodie	$120
T-Shirt	$50
Basics Collection T-Shirt	$35
Beanie	$25
Keychain	$8

BTS

ITEM	PRICE
Ticket - Low Price	$141
Ticket - Average Price	$299
Ticket - High Price (near stage)	$6,249
T-Shirt	$20.99
Sweatshirt	$38
Backpack	$46.99
Baseball Cap	$12.65
Plush Slippers	$22.99
Keychain	$16.99

POST MALONE

ITEM	PRICE
Ticket - Low Price	$71
Ticket - Average Price	$214
Ticket - High Price	$765
VIP Ticket	$1,074
T-Shirt	$35
Long Sleeve T-Shirt	$50
Hoodie	$65
Beanie	$30
Tote Bag	$15
Keychain	$15

TRAVIS SCOTT

ITEM	PRICE
Ticket - Low Price	$40
Ticket - Average Price	$123
Ticket - High Price	$1,181
T-Shirt	$64.99
Long Sleeve	$65
Hoodie	$150
Running Shoes	$136.63
Baseball Cap	$84.47
Phone Case	$46.41
Backpack	$111.79

Sources: The above prices were identified from multiple sources and may no longer be current. Please check retailers for current prices.

BIRTHDAY GIFTS!

Plugged-In Parent asked teens: "If you had $50 to spend, what would you buy your best friend for their birthday?"

Cash, Books, Gift Cards, Bag, Art Supplies, Clothes, Camera, Anime Merch, Food, Take them out, Candy, Computer Gear, Jewelry, Hoodie, Hair & Nail Salon Visit, Video Game, Whatever they want, Perfume, Makeup, YouTuber Merch, Shoes

"What birthday present do you most wish you could *receive* in 2022?"

A week to hang out with friends, Clothes, Trip, Nothing, Oculus, Senior trip with best friends, Computer, Albums, Drawing Tablet, Shoes, Books, For the love of my life to tell me he loves me too, Concert Tickets, Roadtrip with family, Teddy Bear, Money, Airpods, iPhone, PS5, Nintendo Switch, BTS Merch, Tea Pot, Tattoo, Puppy, Gaming headset, Drivers License, Car, Elden Ring, Nintendo DS, Laptop, Gift Card, For my dad to move back

Source: *Plugged-In Parent Survey of Teens* (2022)

GLOSSARY

Do you ever wonder what your kid is talking (or texting) about? If it sounds like English, but you're just not sure what they mean, maybe this glossary of slang will help you out.

SLANG

Basic: A word to describe someone who likes mainstream things and is considered unoriginal.

Bet: A term for agreement or approval.

Bop: A really good song or beat.

Cancel: To stop supporting something or someone by boycotting their work, products, or unfollowing on social media.

Cap: Something that's considered false, most commonly used in the phrase "no cap," which means "no lie."

Catch these hands: To start a fight, typically used in a confrontational matter.

Cheugy: Describes millennials who are trying too hard to be trendy.

Deadass: Seriously or for real.

Drag: To criticize or make fun of something.

Drip: A cool or trendy sense of style. When someone has good drip, people will hype them up by having them do a "drip check," which is showing off your outfit.

GLOSSARY

Fam: A shortened term for "family" typically used to describe one's inner circle.

Finesse: The act of getting what you want by manipulating someone.

Ghosted: To stop communicating with someone out of the blue.

Glow up: To go through a positive physical, mental, or spiritual transformation.

High key: The opposite of "low key," commonly used when you want to emphasize something.

Hits different: Used to describe something that stands out from the rest.

I'm dead: An expression used when you find something hilarious.

It's the ___ for me: Used to describe something that stands out about a person or thing, either positively or negatively.

Iykyk: Stands for "If you know, you know." Used to describe an inside joke or something a certain community would understand.

Karen: A pejorative term for an obnoxious, angry, entitled, middle-aged white woman who uses her privilege to get her way or police other people's behaviors. Karen is generally stereotyped as having a blonde bob haircut, asking to speak to retail and restaurant managers to voice complaints or make demands.

Living rent free: When you can't stop thinking about something.

GLOSSARY

Main character: Someone described as a "main character" tends to be well-liked, confident, and knows they're in control of their life.

"OK, boomer": A put-down used to dismiss something done or said by anyone over the age of 35–40. (Even though actual Baby Boomers are between 57 and 75 years old).

Periodt: A more intense version of "period," meant to add emphasis to the point being made.

Pressed: Being mad or upset about something.

Say less: An expression that means: I get it; no further explanation needed, shut up, or I agree.

Sending me: A term to describe how funny you find something.

Sheesh: Used to hype someone up when they look good or do something good, like saying damn.

Simp: When someone publicly pours their heart out for someone, whether they know the person or not, or goes above and beyond for their significant other.

Sis: A shortened version of "sister" typically used as an affectionate greeting for a close friend.

Skrt: A description of the sound tires make when you leave in a hurry. Used as either an expression of excitement, humor, or to abruptly turn in another direction when not interested.

Slaps: An adjective that describes how great something is.

Snack: A term to describe someone you think is good-looking.

Snatched: A term to describe something that looks really good, typically when it comes to style.

GLOSSARY

Stan: Another word for someone who's a super fan, and often overly enthusiastic of, a celebrity's work.

Sus: Short for "suspicious." It typically means something is not as it may seem.

Tea: Another word for gossip.

Understood the assignment: When someone does a specific activity well.

Vibe: The mood or emotional state someone has.

Vibe check: A pass/no pass situation that checks someone's energy or personality. Can be a permanent thing, or just based on something someone does.

Wig: An expression used when something completely blows you away, referring to the fact that if you had a wig on, it would fly off your head.

Yeet: Two meanings: 1) A word that's an exclamation of approval or excitement. 2) To describe a powerful throw.

EMOJIS

: Feeling shy when complimenting someone or asking for something.

✏️ : Taking mental notes, like noting something on a tutorial video. Often used after each word in a sentence.

📈 / 📉 : To increase or decrease something, or talk about someone or something's popularity after an event.

👁️👄👁️ : In complete shock or unsure how to respond.

GLOSSARY

❗: Makes a word or phrase seem fancy or excited. Also can make a statement stand out.

😬: Although a smiley face, actually used for an awkward situation.

😭: Any dramatic emotion that can mean sadness, anger, happiness, excitement, or feeling overwhelmed.

Sources: *Reader's Digest*, *USA Today*, Lifehacker, Dictionary.com, and Urban Dictionary

GAMER JARGON

AAA/triple A titles: Game titles that have the highest development budgets and massive promotion campaigns. It's similar to the classification of Hollywood movies. Examples of AAA game titles include games such as Asssassin's Creed, Grand Theft Auto, Final Fantasy, Call of Duty, Mass Effect.

AFK: Away from keyboard. Typing AFK in a game chat lets your teammates know that you won't be available to play for a while.

Aggro: When a neutral mob becomes hostile and tries to attack you like Minecraft's Zombie Pigman or Enderman.

Aimbot/bot : A cheat that some players use as an advantage against others in shooter games. Your weapon will automatically aim at another player to achieve the best K/D.

Backwards compatibility: The ability to play games for older consoles on the newest ones. For example, Xbox is slowly releasing Xbox 360 games that can now be played on Xbox One without having to buy them again.

GLOSSARY

Boss: A tough enemy usually found at the end of the level or a game. You have to use every skill that you learned during the previous gameplay.

Camper: A person who sits in one spot for a long time, waiting for other players to find them.

Checkpoint: Specific point where the gameplay is auto saved.

Cross-platform games: Video games that you can play with your friends even if you're not on the same platform. Some of the more well known cross-platform games include Gears of War 4 (Windows 10/Xbox One), Ark: Survival Evolved (Windows 10/Xbox One), Rocket League (Linux/Mac/Xbox One/Steam/PS4).

DDoS attack: Stands for distributed denial of service attack. These types of malicious cyberattacks are aimed at overwhelming the server by using traffic from multiple sources. That way legitimate players are unable to connect and play.

Deathmatch: A gameplay mode in various shooter games where players fight each other until someone wins the most kills.

DLC: Stands for downloadable content. Usually a separate side-story to the main game but can also include content like clothes, skins, or new guns. Some DLCs can also include the entire plot of the original game. Some cost money, some are free.

eSports: A form of competition using video games in multi-player events. eSports games range from shooter games like Battlefield, Overwatch, Halo and Unreal Tournament, sports games like FIFA and Rocket League, to strategy games like League of Legends and Dota.

GLOSSARY

FPS/TPS: First-person shooter is a game played from the character's point of view. Examples include Battlefield, Call of Duty, Counter Strike, Halo, and Overwatch. In third-person shooters you can see the character you're controlling, either where the character is centered or looking over the character's shoulder. Third-person shooters include Resident Evil 4, Gears of War, Tomb Raider, and Assassin's Creed. There are some games where you can switch between these modes, most notably PlayerUnknown's Battlegrounds.

FTW: For the win. This term is usually used when someone does something great.

Get Rekt/Git Rekt: Intentionally misspelled "get wrecked."

GG: Short for good game, usually said after any match, regardless if it was won or lost.

Git gud/get gud: Intentionally misspelled "get good," generally said to inexperienced gamers.

Griefer/griefing: A player who makes other players' online gaming experience miserable by destroying the environment, or killing the player. Notable example is Minecraft, where griefers often destroy other people's houses and other builds.

Grind/mine/farm: Doing the same thing over and over again to get skills, experience points, or better loot.

HP: The health of a player's character is often measured by health or hit points.

HUD: Head-up display showing all the necessary information like a character's health, map, chat, weapons, etc.

K/D: Kill/death ratio in shooter games.

GLOSSARY

Lag: The delay between a player's action and the server's response time.

Loot/drop: Items, currency, or experience that can be obtained several ways in game, either by killing enemies, finding treasure, or picking stuff off the ground.

MMORPG: Massively multiplayer online role-playing game contains a huge online world (usually fantasy or sci-fi related) and a large number of players interacting together. Best known example is World of Warcraft.

Mob/Mobs: Refers to computer controlled living entities. It's short for "mobile."

MOBA: Multiplayer online battle arena video games. Examples include League of Legends, Smite, and Dota 2. These games play differently than FPS games. MOBAs are usually a combination of real-time strategy (RTS), action, and role-playing games.

MP/SP: Multi-player/single-player games. These are not mutually exclusive; some games can have both a single-player campaign and online multi-player. Examples include Battlefield, Assassin's Creed, Minecraft, and Rocket League.

Nerf: When an item, character, or skill is decreased in strength.

Noob/noob: Newbie, a person who is not skilled enough yet. Usually used in a derogatory manner. This word has also spread outside the gaming community.

NPC: Non-player character. Usually characters that interact with you in a game, give you tasks, or have information/items you need to further the game.

GLOSSARY

OP: Abbreviation of overpowered. Item, skill, or player who deals a lot of damage with minimal effort.

PvE: Player versus environment. Players fight against computer-controlled enemies. Can be played alone, with AI companions, or online with human companions. Some PvE games are Destiny, Borderlands, Gears of War, and Payday.

PvP: Player versus player. Players fight each other. Examples include PlayerUnknown's Battlegrounds, Rocket League, Battlefield, Counter Strike, Call of Duty, Mortal Kombat, and many others.

Pwn/pwned: Typo of the word "owned," used to describe being completely annihilated by an enemy.

Raid: Term usually used on Twitch when one Twitch streamer sends their audience over to another Twitch streamer after they end their stream.

Rezz: To resurrect/revive a teammate.

RPG: Role-playing game, where the player decides their character's actions and choices. There is no linear gameplay. The player's choices can influence the plot and the ending in various ways. Notable examples include Fallout, Witcher, Skyrim, Deus Ex, or Dragon Age.

RTS: Real-time strategy video games. Notable examples are games like Age of Empires, Starcraft, Supreme Commander, Warcraft, and Command & Conquer.

Rubberbanding: The term for when you move your character but due to high latency, it pulls you back where you were before, regardless of the distance you covered.

GLOSSARY

Spawn: A place where the player (or item) materializes in a game (for the first time or after death). Spawns can be centralized or random; in some cases you can set your own spawn. In Minecraft you can spawn back after death in your bed if you've previously slept in it.

Spawn camper: If the spawn point is common for all people, some players sit by that point and kill players upon joining the game. This is very frowned upon.

Tagged: Having hit/damaged another player. "I've tagged him two times": player got hit two times but is not dead.

Tank: A player who keeps all enemies focused on themselves, protecting their teammates. Usually has strong armor and good weapons.

TP: Teleport. One player can teleport to another place.

Virtual goods: Non-physical objects and money purchased for use in online communities or online games. Including digital gifts and digital clothing for avatars, virtual goods may be classified as services instead of goods and are usually sold by companies that operate social networking services, community sites, or online games.

WASD: Widely used keyboard combination for character movement. W for forward, S for backward, and A and D for strafing.

XP: Experience points. Part of a loot/drop from killing enemies and bosses, you can use them to level up your skills. In Minecraft you can use XP points to improve your items with various abilities.

Source: "Gamer Talk—The Unique Language of Gamers." Geeky Gaming Stuff.

GLOSSARY

STAN CULTURE JARGON

Bop: A really good song or beat.

Cancel: To stop supporting something or someone by boycotting their work, products, or unfollowing on social media.

Drag: To criticize or make fun of something.

Fav/favs: Short for favorite. Used to identify a favorite person, song, item, etc.

Here for: Typically used to describe a concept, person, couple, or TV show you support. People usually say this when something semi-controversial, funny, or new happens. *"I don't know if the rumors are true, but if Emma Chamberlain and Ethan Dolan are dating, I'm here for it."*

Iconic: Typically used to describe recent, highly original, influential, or unique, works of art, artists, performers, style, etc.

Locals: A word used to describe people who aren't down with current trends or social media behavior.

Mutuals: Mutuals are people you follow who follow you back on social media, creating a space to bond over things you both stan.

Reaching: Term used when someone tries to relate one thing to another using completely irrelevant evidence and information.

Shade: Acting in a casual or disrespectful manner towards someone.

Skinny legend: A positive term that praises the person it is meant to describe with no correlation to one's actual weight or body shape.

Snack: A term to describe someone you think is attractive.

GLOSSARY

Snatched: A term to describe something that looks really good, typically when it comes to style.

Soft block: A phrase often used by Twitter users to describe the blocking of another person, used to make the other user force-unfollow you without making it obvious that you blocked them.

Stan Twitter: A section of Twitter that is comprised of cult-like-fandoms that worship popular artists or artist groups. Fans engage socially to online individuals, discuss topics relating to their faves, fan girl/boy over updates on their faves, and compete amongst the different fandoms.

Stan: Another word for someone who's a super fan, and oftern overly enthusiastic of, a celebrity's work.

Tea: Another word for gossip.

Troll: Someone who deliberately pisses people off online to get a reaction.

We/I/you stan: To stan something means to support or "stand up" for it. It can be used as a compliment too.

Sources: *Reader's Digest*, *USA Today*, Lifehacker, Dictionary.com, and Urban Dictionary

FANDOM JARGON

Alternate universe: Often shortened to AU, alternate universe is a concept, typically in fanfiction where characters are imagined to be in different scenarios.

Anti: A person who hates a ship to the point that part of the hatred is their obsession.

GLOSSARY

Buddyslash: The term for slash between characters who are friends, or more often, partners in canon.

Brotp: The term used when describing a pairing platonically, or as friends.

Canon: Used to refer to a pairing or another aspect of the series that is considered to be true to the storyline.

Cargo ship: Ships between a person and an inanimate object.

Cinnamon roll: A character that is very kind and sweet but faces more hardship and suffering than they truly deserve.

Cosplay: Shortened form of "costume play." The art of dressing in costume or imitating characters or creatures in science fiction and fantasy.

Crack ship: A pairing that is considered to be way out there or impossible. Usually between characters who have never met each other or barely interacted.

Crossover ship: A pairing between characters from different medias who have never interacted.

Endgame: Ships that are canon at the end of a series.

Enemyslash: The term for same-sex ships between characters who are canonically enemies.

Fandom: A fandom is a subculture composed of fans characterized by a feeling of empathy and camaraderie with others who share a common interest. Fans typically are interested in even minor details of the objects of their fandom and spend a significant portion of their time and energy involved with their interest, often as a part of a social network with particular practices, differentiating fandom-affiliated people from those with only a casual interest.

GLOSSARY

Fanfiction/fanfic: Fanfiction is when someone takes either the story or characters (or both) of a certain piece of work, whether it be a novel, TV show, movie, etc., and creating their own story based on it.

Fankids: Children of a pairing made up by specific fans and/or the fandom.

Fanon: The opposite of canon, a collection of ideas that is normally used in fanfictions or fandom, but doesn't exist in official canon work.

Fanwork: A creative work created by one or more fans, intended for other fans.

Femslash: Derived from "female slash" refers to relationships between two female characters.

Ghost ship: A ship that you once supported and perhaps still do that went down in the ocean, drowning all on board. Basically, you've given up hope of it becoming canon.

Headcanon: A fan's personal interpretation of canon, including the habits of a character, the backstory of a character, or the nature of relationships between characters.

Meta: Discussion about events or people in canon that provides further insight to the text, most often by the fans and for the fans.

Multishipper: Someone who likes different ships involving the same character(s).

Notp: A ship that one dislikes.

OTP: One True Pairing. Meaning your favorite combination of characters in a fandom.

GLOSSARY

Pairing: The characters who make up the central focus of a fanwork.

Queerbaiting: Creators purposefully putting romantic subtext between same-sex characters into the work without the intention of making the couple canon, with the intention of drawing in a queer audience.

Rarepair: A ship that is extremely uncommon or unpopular within its fandom and doesn't have many fanworks.

Sailed ship: A ship that became canon.

Shipper: Someone who takes part in shipping. A fan is called a "shipper" when they support a relationship, whether it's canon or not.

Ship bait: Intentionally created potential pairings to attract the attention of shippers.

Shipper goggles: When a viewer interprets the smallest, most ambiguous canonical evidence in favor of their ship of choice.

Shipperpression: A depression caused by the end of one's favored ship.

Shipping: Derived from the word relationship, the belief that two characters, fictional or non-fictional, would be interesting or believable (or are, or will be, or should be) in a romantic relationship.

Ship war: A heated disagreement between two or more groups of shippers that spans a long time and involves many people in their fandom.

Side pairing: A pairing that is described in the story, but is not the main focus.

GLOSSARY

Slash: Slash refers to relationships between two male characters. Slash ships are recognizable by the slash, '/' between the characters

Slasher: A fan of slash ships, usually those who write male/male fanfiction.

Slashy: Commonly used to describe relationships between characters of the same gender that can easily be read as sexual or romantic.

Wrongshipping: When a fan ships two characters who really shouldn't be together.

Source: "Shipping Wiki." Fandom.com.

Good Relationships for Your Children Start With You

Secrets To Surviving Your Children's Love Relationships by Terri Orbuch, PhD is a must-read if you want your children to grow up and have healthy, happy relationships of their own.

Learn more at **relationshipsecrets.guide**

Published by
PARENT READY
parentready.com

CONTRIBUTORS

NICK BRACCIA is a Cannes Lions– and Clio–winning writer, director, and producer. He is the author of *Off the Back of a Truck: Unofficial Contraband for the Sopranos Fan* (Tiller Press 2020) and co-author of *Video Palace: In Search of the Eyeless Man: Collected Stories* (Tiller Press 2020). In 2018, he co-created and co-executive produced the horror podcast *Video Palace* for AMC Network's streaming service Shudder. While working at the marketing agency Campfire, he helped to develop immersive, narrative experiences for TV shows like *Outcast*, *Sense8*, *Watchmen*, *The Man in the High Castle*, *Westworld*, and *The Purge*. Braccia is a member of the Producers Guild of America and lives in Manhattan with his partner, Amanda, and daughter, Evie Blue.

TRYSTON BROWN is a 15-year-old high school sophomore who resides in Maryland. He lives and breathes sneakers, is an avid music lover, and feels most at home on the basketball court.

FRANK CARUSO is a cartoonist, creative director and author who has collaborated with Bruce Springsteen on the illustrated book *Outlaw Pete,* based on Springsteen's song of the same name; with Andrew Vachss on the graphic novel *Heart Transplant,* covering the topic of bullying; and is currently collaborating with Green Day on the illustrated book *Last of the American Girls,* based on the band's 2009 song. Caruso is also the creative director for the iconic Betty Boop, has two Emmy Awards in Children's Television, and is a member of New York's Society of Illustrators.

CONTRIBUTORS

NOAH CARUSO currently works in Pop/Rock Promotion at Atlantic Records and has been involved behind-the-scenes in several different facets of the music industry, from live events to radio. Growing up a musician and graduating from St. Joseph's University with a bachelor's in communications and entertainment marketing, his passion for music has constantly been a part of his life—personally, academically, and professionally.

ERIC DEGGANS is NPR's first full-time TV critic, crafting stories and commentaries for the network's shows, such as *Morning Edition, Here & Now,* and *All Things Considered*, along with writing material for NPR.org. He also appears on NPR podcasts such as *Consider This, Life Kit, Code Switch, It's Been a Minute,* and *Pop Culture Happy Hour*. Eric is an adjunct instructor in the Sanford School of Public Policy at Duke University.

MIRANDA GILBERT is a liberal studies MA student at The New School for Social Research, concentrating on gender and sexuality studies and comparative literature. As a researcher, Miranda has done work with academics throughout various disciplines including political science, literature, theory, and more. Following her graduation, Miranda plans to earn a PhD in literature. Having recently started writing a book, Miranda wishes to use her writing to create relationships with publishing houses in hopes of publishing both her work, and helping to publish the work of others whose voices need to be heard.

SUMMER HORVATH was born in Las Vegas, Nevada, where she spent her whole life immersed in music, live events, and radio. After working a concert a week and being a part of every massive event happening in town, she got a job offer to work for Atlantic Records in Los Angeles, CA. By working with A-list artists, endless concerts, and learning the ins and outs of production, she has also found another passion for motivational speaking. By doing this, she has been able to mentor children and young adults to follow their dreams to be the best they can be.

CARRIE JAMES is a research associate and principal investigator at Harvard Graduate School of Education's Project Zero. A sociologist by training, her research explores young people's digital, moral, and civic lives. With Emily Weinstein, Carrie is co-author of the book, *Behind Their Screens: What Teens are Facing (and Adults are Missing)* from The MIT Press, 2022. Carrie's publications also include *Disconnected: Youth, New Media, and the Ethics Gap* (The MIT Press, 2014). She holds a MA (1996) and a PhD (2003) in sociology from New York University. She is the parent of two technology-loving kids, ages 12 and 16. You can follow her on Twitter at @carrie_james.

HENRY JENKINS is the provost professor of Communication, Journalism, Cinematic Arts and Education at the University of Southern California. He is the author and/or editor of 20 books on various aspects of media and popular culture, most recently *Participatory Culture: Interviews, Popular Culture and the Civic Imagination: Case Studies of Creative Social Change,* and *Comics and Stuff.* Jenkins is the principal investigator for The Civic Imagination Project, funded by the MacArthur Foundation, to explore ways to inspire creative collaborations within communities as they work together to identify shared values and visions for the future.

NORA JODREY is a freelance writer. She is also a self-proclaimed running, horse, and science nerd who lives in Washington, DC.

CONTRIBUTORS

ELON JUSTICE is a writer and filmmaker born in Pikeville, KY. A graduate of Western Kentucky University and MIT, her work most often focuses on groups underrepresented in media, rural communities, and more equitable methods of storytelling.

JESSICA MASON lives near Portland, Oregon, with her wife, daughter, and corgi. She is a journalist, podcaster, and author of nonfiction, fiction, and fan fiction. She has written for fan sites across the internet, including The Mary Sue, Bustle, and Decider. She's a *Supernatural* super-fan and literally wrote the book on the show, *The Binge Watcher's Guide To Supernatural* from Riverdale Avenue Books.

TRACEY JAI PANNELL is an eccentric creative specializing in a multitude of subjects. In her spare time, she enjoys customizing garments, reading tarot, creating art of numerous mediums, and of course, watching anime. Tracey believes in the importance of knowledge and sharing alternative perspectives. Her works, whether written or otherwise, are a mirror to her essence.

BECKY PHAM, MA, is a communication researcher who is working on her PhD at the University of Southern California, Annenberg School for Communication and Journalism. She specializes in researching media use and popular culture engagement by parents, children, and youth. She firmly believes in translating academic research for societal benefit. Her writing has appeared in *Psychology Today*. For more information, visit https://beckypham.com/.

ANJA SCHMIDT has been an editor in the book and magazine publishing industries for more than 20 years. She is currently Executive Editor at *Parent Ready* and Executive Managing Editor for *FEEL FREE* magazine.

CONTRIBUTORS

MICHAEL TIMKO is an owner at Fun Stuff Toys based in Seaford, NY. Fun Stuff Toys is celebrating its 35th year in business!

DR. EMILY WEINSTEIN is a senior researcher at Project Zero and a lecturer at the Harvard Graduate School of Education. Dr. Weinstein studies the intersections of networked technologies with the social, emotional, and civic lives of adolescents and emerging adults. Her first book, *Behind Their Screens: What Teens Are Facing (And Adults Are Missing)*, is forthcoming from The MIT Press (Weinstein & James, 2022). In Spring 2022, she is teaching a new course, Digital Dilemmas: Adolescents Behind Their Screens. Dr. Weinstein holds a master's degree (EdM) in prevention science and practice and a doctorate (EdD) in human development and education, both from Harvard University, and a BS from Cornell University.

The College Ready Series

"The transition to college isn't just about your student. This step-by-step guide offers tips for a successful first year for the whole family."

Marjorie Savage
Author of *You're on Your Own (But I'm Here If You Need Me): Mentoring Your Child During the College Years*

Written by expert university family relation leaders, the *College Ready* series prepares parents and students for each unique year of college. *College Ready 2023* is also available as a Spanish edition.

"*Post-College Ready* is chock-full of helpful advice as families help college seniors launch into life off campus."

W. Houston Dougharty
Special Advisor to the President, Formerly Vice President for Student Affairs, Hofstra University

Available June 2023!

Learn more at **collegeready.guide**

Published by

parentready.com

www.ingramcontent.com/pod-product-compliance
Lightning Source LLC
Chambersburg PA
CBHW061649040426
42446CB00010B/1663